Praise for

Mastering the Mental Game of Trading

"What I LOVE, LOVE, LOVE about this book from Steven is that it helps you sharpen your mental game by sharing entertaining and enlightening real-world stories from his 25 years of trading experience and then coaching traders. This is a special book of trading wisdom that needs to sit on your bookshelf."

—Mike Bellafiore, co-founder of SMB Capital and SMB Training

"I have known Steven for many years; he is the best trading coach I've seen. He's also an excellent writer who can seamlessly mix compelling stories and practical information. His real-world trading experience, his years of coaching, and his ability to communicate clearly make *Mastering the Mental Game of Trading* one of the most important trading books in years.

Mastering the Mental Game of Trading is full of actionable advice, useful models, and powerful frameworks for thinking that will help you master both your outer and inner trading game. Steven's decades of experience, his empathy, and his expert coaching and trading knowledge make this book an instant must-read. I strongly recommend it for traders of every experience level."

—Brent Donnelly, author of *Alpha Trader* and *The Art of Currency Trading*

"An inspiring and thought-provoking book that uniquely views trading performance and alpha generation through the lens of purpose, presence and process. The journey through the book is vividly brought to life by Steve's own front-line trading experience and the stories of many others. Essential reading!"

—Mark Randall, market veteran, performance coach and co-host of the *AlphaMind* podcast

"This wonderfully written book demands thoughtful introspection. It is a far cry from the cookie-cutter coaching books and instead encompasses a life philosophy for traders. It unravels the intricate relationship between emotions, decision-making and financial success in the world of trading. I could read it once a month – it is that enjoyable!"

—Linda Raschke, renowned trader featured in Jack Schwager's *New Market Wizards*

"Steven Goldstein's experience encompasses both a 25-year career as a proprietary trader and a second career as a highly regarded trading coach. In fact, several of the best traders I have ever interviewed have engaged Steven as their trading coach. Most traders don't realize that the inner game of trading (the disciplined control of one's mental state) is as critical to success as the outer game of trading (the strategy and its execution). Traders typically fail because of a deficient or non-existent inner game rather than due to a poor outer game. In *Mastering the Mental Game of Trading*, Steven Goldstein guides the reader through the process of integrating the inner and outer games of trading. The lessons of the book are brought to life through actual trading anecdotes drawn from both Steven's own experience and those of the traders he has coached."

—Jack Schwager, author of the *Market Wizards* book series

"Steven's easy to read book deftly addresses the most important subject in creating sustained success – what goes on in your head. He adroitly tackles the complexities of developing an effective strategy for the ultimate edge in any endeavor – the mental game. As one of the few performance coaches who first traded for his living, Steven is a mental coach whose words should have weight in any trader's arsenal."

—**Denise Shull, leading performance coach for hedge funds and professional athletes, author of *Market Mind Games***

"In his book *Mastering the Mental Game of Trading*, Steven Goldstein first lays a foundation for understanding the "inner" and "outer" aspects of trading, explaining the interplay of the trader's ego and self. He then shows how this interplay depends on the specific trading game that we're playing and the phase of the performance cycle we are currently in. Filled with real-world examples of mental game mastery and specific strategies for achieving that mastery, this book is a valuable resource for beginning traders and experienced money managers alike."

—**Brett N. Steenbarger, PhD, professor of psychiatry and behavioral sciences at SUNY Upstate Medical University and author of *The Psychology of Trading: Tools and Techniques for Minding the Markets*, and several other major books**

MASTERING THE MENTAL GAME OF TRADING

Every owner of a physical copy of this edition of

MASTERING THE MENTAL GAME OF TRADING

can download the eBook for free direct from us at Harriman House, in a DRM-free format that can be read on any eReader, tablet or smartphone.

Simply head to:

ebooks.harriman-house.com/ mastermentalgametrading

to get your copy now.

MASTERING THE MENTAL GAME OF TRADING

Harnessing the power of the inner self to fuel trading outperformance

STEVEN GOLDSTEIN

HARRIMAN HOUSE LTD
3 Viceroy Court
Bedford Road
Petersfield
Hampshire
GU32 3LJ
GREAT BRITAIN
Tel: +44 (0)1730 233870
Email: enquiries@harriman-house.com
Website: harriman.house

First published in 2024.

Paperback ISBN: 978-1-80409-007-7
eBook ISBN: 978-1-80409-008-4

British Library Cataloguing in Publication Data
A CIP catalogue record for this book can be obtained from the British Library.

I dedicate this book to my late sister Joanne Goldstein (1967 to 2001), my best friend for the first twenty years of my life. Jo was a special person and inspiration taken from us, and this world, much too young.

CONTENTS

ACKNOWLEDGEMENTS

I am deeply grateful for the incredible individuals who have played significant roles in this journey. Although there are too many to mention individually, I would like to express my immense gratitude to some key people.

First and foremost, I want to thank my amazing wife, Lisa (aka Lisa-Lou), for her unwavering support throughout my journey as a trader and coach. She has been my rock and has stood by me through it all, including the entire writing process of this book. I could not have accomplished any of this without her strength and support. I am also grateful to my wonderful daughters, Gaby and Holly, who have endured my occasional moods and have grown into inspirational individuals in their own right. I cannot thank them enough. Lastly, I would like to express my appreciation to Ollie, whose presence since coming on the scene has often lifted my spirits.

I dedicated this book to my sister, Jo, who was my best friend for most of my life until her sudden departure. Although her loss deeply affected our family, it also revealed the profound strength and character of my parents. Witnessing their resilience has had a profound impact on me and has been an inspiration to our entire family.

Navigating the world of markets can be challenging, but the friendships I have formed along the way have been instrumental in both surviving and thriving. While it is impossible to name everyone, I would like to extend my heartfelt appreciation to a few remarkable individuals.

My oldest friend in the markets, Sue, the petrolhead from down-under, has been a constant presence and sounding board throughout this journey. Spike (Richard Vater), my market-brother, has always been there with a sharp wit and a much-needed put-down should I get ahead of myself. Justin, my broker turned close friend, and Bill, another broker and my very first coaching client, have all made life a little easier and a lot more fun.

Lifelong friends from my days at Credit Suisse, including Yasser, DJ, Hatchy, Markey G, Tony, Simon, Alan, and others with whom I may have lost touch, have been a great source of support. Likewise, I want to acknowledge those from Amex, particularly Ash, whose impact is felt throughout this book, and the unstoppable Shep. I am also grateful to Karen 'Kazza' Jones, a brilliant technical analyst who followed me from Credit Suisse to Commerzbank, and all those at the Society of Technical Analysts, who have been unwavering supporters of my work.

My gratitude extends to my peers in coaching, Peter Burditt being foremost among them. I owe him an immeasurable debt of gratitude for catalysing my growth as a trader and inspiring me to become a coach. I also want to express my thanks to my AlphaMind collaborator, Mark Randall, for his unwavering support and insightful contributions throughout the writing process.

Numerous exceptional teachers have influenced me on this journey, notably Sally Denham-Vaughan and Marie-Anne Chidiac 'MAC,' whose insights from Gestalt have permeated this book. Maria Illiffe-Wood, my book coach, whom I met at the Welwyn Garden City Co-Coaching forum, has been instrumental in my coaching journey, alongside the incredible fellow coaches in the WGC group.

I must express my heartfelt thanks to the team at Harriman House, particularly Craig Pearce, for their unwavering support and guidance throughout the writing process. Special mention goes to Nick Fletcher for his expert editing, which transformed my appalling English into legible content.

While I cannot mention them individually, I extend a massive thank you to all the traders and client organisations I have worked with over the years. I could continue with more acknowledgments, but this would turn into a book of its own.

FOREWORD BY PETER BURDITT

I HAD THE PLEASURE of coaching Steven almost a quarter of a century ago when he was a trader at a leading investment bank. A decade later he and I met up again, and I told him that with his understanding of the market, his industry expertise, and moreover his strong ethical compass, he was the perfect candidate to pursue a future as a trader coach. Having been global head of markets strategy myself for a top UK investment bank, and having later trained in Gestalt psychology and coaching traders, I knew what a rewarding career it was to help traders realise their full potential.

And I have been proved right!

Over the years I have had the pleasure of witnessing Steven's transformation from a successful trader to an exceptional performance coach. Acting initially as his mentor and supervisor, in recent years I have had the privilege of partnering with him on numerous coaching projects. I am honoured and delighted to provide a foreword for Steven's book. He offers an unparalleled perspective on the themes that prevent traders reaching their full potential and how to unlock them.

I have witnessed first-hand how our innate pathologies, emotions, heuristical biases, and rigid egos can significantly impact and hinder performance. This is exacerbated by the unpredictability and volatility of financial markets which offer a mirror to a trader's mindset. The mastery of our mind is the key differentiator that separates an average trader who merely punches the tickets from an extraordinary trader, one who reads the market consistently, weathers the storms with courage and perseverance and sets the stage for exceptional performance. Developing the ability to remain calm and focused against the daily challenges of uncertainty is the cornerstone of success. In working with traders for over 25 years, I know that the processes Steven uses change people's lives. This is why I am excited that he has taken the time to write this book to share his successful techniques with a wider audience.

In *Mastering the Mental Game of Trading*, Steven offers a unique perspective on how traders can improve their mental game and achieve greater success. Drawing upon his extensive experience, both as a trader in the hot seat and as a trading performance coach working with some of the best in the industry, he shares practical steps and insights that can help traders develop greater self-awareness, overcome emotional biases, and become more objective in their decision-making. How many times have we heard traders complain that the market is wrong? The market is never wrong, it is our mindset in successfully riding the waves that is not right!

By introducing his powerful Performance Process Cycle model, Steven provides traders with an actionable framework that identifies their strengths and weaknesses, which results in their improvement. Using real-life examples, he shows how his model can help traders navigate the challenges of the trading world with greater confidence, agility and success.

Trading in financial markets is an exciting and rewarding endeavour, but it's not easy. It requires a unique set of skills, knowledge, personal mastery and experience to succeed. In a world of diminishing margins, increased computerisation and unparalleled volatility, today, more than ever, traders need to develop high-performance skills to navigate the fast-paced and ever-changing landscape of the markets.

As you read this book, I encourage you to reflect on your own attitudes and behaviours, and to embrace the insights and guidance that Steven provides.

Peter Burditt

Peter Burditt is a senior associate member of the Royal Society of Medicine, an APECS accredited master coach, founder of Strategic Development Consultants Ltd and an FCCA (retired).

INTRODUCTION

THIS BOOK IS about *you*.

Like most traders, you probably know intuitively that the activity you are engaged in is fundamentally a mental game, fought mostly in that space that exists between your left brain and your right brain, and pitting you the trader against your self in a psychological battle.

To truly excel as a trader, you must conquer these internal psychological challenges while at the same time facing the external challenges presented by the markets, and your ability to navigate them successfully. Mastery of this psychological battle, the mental game, is the key to achieving exceptional performance and reaching the success you desire in trading. This starts with gaining a deeper understanding of the mental game of trading, and then learning how to master it.

Ground zero for this mental game is the relationship you have with your self. As human beings, we go through a constant ebb and flow of emotions when it comes to our own sense of worth – on the one hand, we might possess unwavering faith and confidence in ourselves, while on the other hand, we grapple with creeping doubts, insecurities, and our own personal inner demons. This tumultuous relationship is one that many can relate to, and it forms the foundation of our daily struggles and triumphs.

In the volatile, uncertain, and complex world of markets, we often think the answers to the challenges we face in the market, lie out there.

We seek more knowledge, better insights, deeper analysis, faster news, additional research, the opinions of others, different behaviours and new skills; and yet all along, the most powerful answers lie within. It is within ourselves, where our power and potential lies.

You, and your self can do amazing things when you have each other's back, when you and your self are aligned, working towards the same purpose, trusting one another, backing one another, and being compassionate in support of each other, you and your self can be an amazing team, each other's number one ally. When you do so, you can win the mental game.

But it's not easy, the mental game happens largely below the level of consciousness, in an arena, the markets, which often pitch you against yourself, for their own benefit. They don't want you winning, because if you do, they don't.

I have been that trader who fought that mental game for many years. Though I suspected that the answer was within, I kept searching for it *out there*. This search proved to be fruitless and led me down a familiar path of repeating the same instinctive patterns of behaviour, the same habitual responses, and feeling the same internal frustrations.

Eventually, a fortunate set of circumstances took me on a different route.

This new path involved a journey of self-discovery, a journey into myself, a journey to find out who I was. From that point on, my fortunes as a trader changed significantly.

Later, that path took another turn, towards a new career as a performance coach working with traders. I started getting up close and personal with other people's internal challenges. I helped them to look inwards, to drive better performance by helping them discover their selves in the context of their trading, so that they too could start to understand and improve their own mental game.

This book aims to shed light on this internal conflict, using models, ideas and stories from my own and other traders' experiences of how the conflict manifests in people's work as traders. As you read it, I encourage you to reflect on your own inner battles and to think of what and how you could start to change in ways that help you emerge from them victorious. Winning these battles is what mastering the mental game of trading is all about.

This book is about *you*.

HOW TO READ THIS BOOK

Mastering the Mental Game of Trading is not a book of answers, and while it *is* a trading book, it is not a book *about* trading. Rather, it is a book about you, the trader; or you, the performer, if your world is not trading. Its learnings are applicable in all walks of life, all areas of performance, all fields of practice. It is a book of awareness-raising. As we become more self-aware, we become more conscious of the discrepancies between our selves and the way we are acting and behaving. This enables us to become more conscious of how we are in the moment, even in the face of difficult and conflicting emotions. This in turn empowers us to start responding in ways that give us greater ownership over our behaviours, decisions and actions. Heightened self-awareness is ultimately restorative and healing. It drives better, more effective and more productive performance in whatever endeavour you are engaged in.

As you progress through the pages of this book, you will be introduced to thought-provoking models and new perspectives on trading and markets. These are supported by real traders' stories, as well as my own experiences from almost 25 years as a trader for institutions such as Credit Suisse, Commerzbank, and American Express Bank, followed by more than a decade working as a coach.

The purpose of this book is to catalyse your own reflections so that you become more aware of your own mental game. I encourage you to proceed with curiosity and an open mind. Try to challenge and question your own thinking; you might discover things about yourself that can help you master your own mental game.

Part One of the book, Chapters 1 to 7, serves as an introduction to the fundamental aspects that underpin its themes. Key concepts, ideas, and models essential to the book are introduced here, with the 'Performance Process Cycle' serving as the primary framework. The Performance Process Cycle outlines the various stages of a trader's process, emphasizing how navigating the unpredictability of financial markets can impact their psyche and subsequent behaviour.

Another critical concept in the foundational section is the 'Two Trading Approaches' model, which distinguishes between two related but opposing types of trading. The model encourages traders to reflect on their approach, risk process and mindset to assess whether they align with the type of trading they practise. Together with other ideas raised, these concepts provide a robust foundation for the book, setting the stage for further exploration.

Each of Parts 2 to 5 takes a deep dive into one of the four quadrants of the Performance Process Cycle, using stories and examples that bring to life the concepts and ideas introduced in the foundational section. These sections add flesh to the bones of the Performance Process Cycle.

Many of the stories used in this book are taken from my experiences and the experiences of my clients, because I believe this is the best way to convey my findings in a way that you, the reader, can relate to and empathise with. Yet as a coach I have to guarantee confidentiality and discretion to my clients and their employers. While my clients have given me permission to share these stories, the identities of those involved have been anonymised, as have the contexts in which the stories are set, to ensure full confidentiality is honoured.

In the first chapter of this book, you will be introduced to the intricate idea of the self and the various internal struggles that arise between our genuine core self and our ego. The chapter delves deeper into how our ego's negative influence can hamper our efforts to achieve self-mastery. By delving into this crucial topic, the chapter highlights a practical example from my personal journey, emphasising the self-challenge that traders, performers, and individuals in high performance environments face.

PART ONE

FOUNDATIONAL ELEMENTS

CHAPTER 1

The Mental Game – Mastering Your Self, the Key To Trading Mastery

It is not the mountain we conquer, but ourselves.

Sir Edmund Hillary, mountaineer

THE JOURNEY HOME from my trading job at a bank in the heart of London was more unpleasant than usual. It was summer 2007. The train was crowded, hot and sticky; and there was nowhere to sit. This was not helped by the fact that the two previous trains were cancelled, as always seemed to happen on the hottest days on the Thameslink service.

As I stood on the train, I contemplated a conversation I'd had with my colleague, Ashley, at my trading desk earlier that day.

It had started with me throwing my pen down in frustration, cursing and kicking-out in anger, as the market started to gather speed in the wrong direction.

"You're doing it again," I heard Ashley say.

"What?" I said brusquely, as I turned to him.

"You know, that thing where you start beating yourself up."

"Oh, that. Well you would do the same if you were half the idiot I am," I said, just proving his point.

Then he said something that didn't really land with me at the time, but which I later contemplated as I stood on the train.

"I just don't get it," he said, before pausing to take a sip of his four-shot Starbucks Americano. "You sit here every year with no customers, no client flow, no obvious edge, and yet every year you make money. Every year, without fail, you produce profit from nothing. It's like you're an alchemist. If I had that ability, the last thing I would do is beat myself up."

Ashley was not someone who generally heaped praise on others or showed compassion. He was a great mate, and like great mates we spent most days ribbing each other and bantering. Serious conversations were rare – or even, close to non-existent.

I looked at him, but before I could respond, a shout from one of my brokers disturbed the moment. I turned back to the screens, the profound comment from Ashley now lost in the mayhem of markets.

Several hours later, on that train, Ashley's comments had made their way back into my consciousness.

"An Alchemist," he had said. He was right. I had no flow, no customers, no margin or spread to capture. The trading seat at the bank was not part of a franchise, and thus had no inherent value. There were no gifts that came my way. The risk appetite of the bank I worked at was best summed up as, "Trade, but don't lose money," and I never did. I started with nothing, yet always ended up with something considerable. That's quite an ability when you think about it.

Then my mind turned to another comment from Ashley: "You know, that thing where you start beating yourself up."

I reflected on that.

Being beaten up, both physically and mentally, does things to your mental state. It undermines you, weakens you, puts you 'in your place.' It makes you fearful and keeps you afraid, changes your behaviour, causes you to hide and not take risks, to act meekly from a place of fear. It depletes your mental capital.

I was doing all of those things to myself. I was undermining myself. I was getting in my own way.

Taking on the market – playing the 'outer' game against an external opponent – is hard enough at the best of times. It becomes a lot harder when you are undermining your self by losing the 'inner' game within your mind at the same time.

I hung up my professional trading gloves in 2010, after nearly 25 years. I made a choice to indulge my other passion – helping people – by deciding to focus on developing myself as a performance coach for traders.

I continued to trade, though as a side hobby rather than a serious venture.

My new career gave me the time and opportunity to reflect on many of my trading activities. The conversations I went on to have with traders from all manner of backgrounds would spark recollections of many of my experiences that now, with the sort of distance that time gives you, enabled me to view these with a rare degree of clarity.

I have reflected regularly on that conversation with Ashley and on how I would "beat myself up," as he put it. I've thought about the negative spiral I was in, and how a few simple words from a colleague helped me to find a way out of it on that occasion.

As traders, we can easily lose ourselves in our trading and often get in the way of ourselves. Exiting this negative pattern is simple in theory, yet so difficult in practice.

In the moment, I was unable to see how lost I had become, but with greater self-awareness I could have extricated myself from that state much earlier. The reality is that most of the time we are blind to ourselves in the moment.

That does not need to be the case for you.

CONQUERING OURSELVES

My behaviour was not something unique to trading or investing. It demonstrated a core part of the human condition and a feature of all high-performance activities, from sport to music, acting to martial arts, leadership and entrepreneurship to acts of endeavour.

Success in all performance activities relies on developing mastery over your self. Self-mastery is the objective of the mental game.

The mental game of trading occurs at the nexus of two distinct yet interconnected games: your inner game, where you strive for self-mastery, and your outer game, where you face the market as you navigate your external environment. How you fare in the outer game affects your inner game, making it essential to maintain balance between these two aspects of trading.

Your inner game is played in your mind and is the foundation block your outer game rests upon. A weak and fractured inner game will not sustain an outer game, no matter how strong it appears.

Your inner game relies on the quality of the relationship you have with your self – the relationship between you and your ego.

As you engage in your outer game, your relationship with your self gets sorely tested. Doubt your self, fail to believe in your self, fail to back and trust your self at key moments, and your ability to execute your outer game effectively will be severely compromised.

Equally, if you over-value your self, or have such levels of self-belief that failure is not in your lexicon, your inner game will be too rigid in the face of ground-shaking tremors. When this happens, it will inevitably collapse. A degree of fragility is a good thing!

YOUR RELATIONSHIP WITH YOUR SELF

The quality and nature of your relationship with your self lies at the heart of your mental game. There are two parts to you which we shall focus on through this book. Your 'self' and your 'ego'.

The ego is often a difficult concept to fully understand, let alone describe. Even in the world of psychology, people have not settled on its exact meaning, or in some cases, whether it even exists. Rather than attempt to provide a comprehensive definition, over the next few pages I will explore the practical ways in which the ego differs from the self and clarify its significance in a way that hopefully will resonate with you.

The ego gets a bad wrap in trading. On the face of it, this is deserved. Careers can be destroyed when a person's ego betrays them, sabotaging their ability to stick to a successful process.

Traders are often told to leave their egos at the door of the trading room. But being able to do that is as realistic as separating yourself from your shadow. Your ego, like your shadow, travels with you wherever you go.

Let us expand on this analogy by imagining that your work relied on you not being betrayed by your shadow.

You would seek to understand your shadow, and you would try to gain a greater understanding of how your shadow impacts your work. You would then make adjustments to how you work, finding ways to work with your shadow so that it does not corrupt your ability to work effectively.

This might sound abstract, but more jobs depend on our shadows than you might think. Hunters, soldiers, spies, police (when following a suspect) – all require a firm working relationship with their shadow.

Now let us apply the same thinking to your ego.

What should you do if your work could be undermined by your ego?

This is of course a rhetorical question – I don't expect you to know the answer at this point. Few people do, and fewer still do anything about it. They carry on regardless.

I am going to up the ante on this question. The quality of your relationship with your self, which is impacted by your ego, is significantly more important to your chances of success in trading than any company results, decisions of central bank policy-makers, announcements, chart formations, or data releases.

There is an alternative perspective to consider with the ego, though this rarely gets aired much in the self-help litany. Think of any great sportsperson, actor, comedian, musician, leader or entrepreneur.

None of them achieved what they did without being driven to succeed by their ego.

We can say the same about masters of the academic worlds, scientists, engineers. They had to impose their ego and their will on others to break through barriers and overturn established ideas.

Changing people's minds and attitudes does not happen by itself, it needs people to drive it. Nelson Mandela, Mahatma Gandhi, Martin Luther King Jr, Lech Wałęsa and other titans of liberation movements could not have enabled momentous change if their egos had not encouraged them to project themselves.

The ego works both ways. It has a bright side and a dark side. Working successfully with your ego – not banishing it or silencing it – leads to victory. Your ego requires balance, understanding and taming. Not too much, but not too little either.

When the great pit trader Marty Schwartz said: "The most important change in my trading career occurred when I learned to divorce my ego from the trade," he had learned to tame his ego. He hadn't banished it. The purpose of this book is to help you move towards achieving mastery of your mental game, by enabling you to strive towards attaining this state.

WORKING WITH YOUR EGO

The ego is neither your enemy nor your ally. It is just a part of you that functions in the background – a part of you with a job to do. Think of it as a virtual, metaphysical organ. Just as you need your physical organs for healthy bodily functioning, your ego is needed to ensure a healthy mental state. Each organ has its own job to do, and each must remain in balance to work effectively. The ego is no different.

From an evolutionary perspective, the purpose of the ego is to be your 'relational guardian'. It seeks to ensure safety in your relationships with others in your world, and with aspects of the world around you.

The ego can be considered a legacy of our ancient primate operating system, and perhaps even older mammalian operating systems. For our primate ancestors, the ego's role was to help its host avoid rejection and then ejection from its social group.

Ejection was an existential threat – potentially a death sentence. If a primate was ejected from a group, it had to be accepted by another group quickly, otherwise its survival was unlikely.

The ego worked to ensure its host primate acted to retain the approval of its fellow group members or, if ejected, would be accepted by another group.

The ego remains a central feature of how we operate and function. Even though the process of evolution has changed us a great deal, we remain social and relational beings who need the support and approval of others. "No man is an island," remains as true now as it was when John Donne stated as far back as the 17th century.

The ego steers its host towards acting in ways that win the admiration of its peers. The ego wants its host to be respected. It wants its host to maintain its sense of identity, so it can identify with its peers and they with it. It wants its host to be promoted within the peer group, making ejection less likely and ensuring the group provides it with security.

To do this the ego uses a system of rewards and punishments distributed through the body's nervous system. When it senses a favourable outcome, it sends rewards in the form of positive neurochemicals which make us feel joyful, happy, even elated.

The moment the ego detects an unfavourable outcome – one that may be a threat to its host's standing and status – it sends a shot of negative neurochemicals through its host's nervous system. These seek to make the host attentive to these threats and ensure it takes action to earn the favour and support of the group.

The ego values security and dislikes uncertainty, since this makes it vulnerable to negative outcomes. Safety is not 'the absence of threat', it is the ability to connect with others and have their support.

The neurochemicals we receive from our ego contribute to our mood, our state, our decisions and our behaviours. They give rise to the emotions that make us jittery, jumpy, fearful, nervous, anxious.

One minute your trade is in the money, and the neurochemicals you are sent make you feel like a king. Seconds later the trade drops deep into the red, and you receive new neurochemicals that make you feel like a clown.

The ego has an agenda whereby it wants you to be admired and liked. This agenda is great when it aligns to the task you want to succeed in. Making money will win you praise from your managers, team members, stakeholders, and your self of course.

However, when the ego is not aligned to your task, its role as guardian can become problematic. In these incidents it tries to take control of your actions. It is in doing this that it ends up sabotaging you in your attempts to fulfil your task. This is self-sabotage. This will be fleshed out later in the book, but a simple example of it occurs when traders interfere with a planned trade, because they fear losing gains or making losses. The ego wants the praise, and thus overrides the trader's process.

Engaging in a battle of wills with your ego is common, but it's not a fair fight. If your ego triumphs, you'll turn against your self, and your potential will be limited. If you triumph, and succeed in defeating your ego, your ego is not down and out. Such victories are only ever temporary. You can never truly beat your ego.

However, you should remember that your true self is capable of great things once it has learned what to do and has the freedom to pursue it.

As traders, it's essential to continually fight the battle to tame our egos, as Marty Schwartz did. Only by doing so can you succeed in the mental game of trading, and ultimately succeed in trading. Those who master this skill learn to contain their egos and stay focused on trading, while using their ego as motivation to achieve success.

In the next chapter, I will introduce you to the Performance Process Cycle, the main model of this book, which aims to help you take control of this fight with the ego, and which in many other ways can empower you to overcome the various challenges which can undermine you as you play the mental game of trading.

CHAPTER 2

Introducing the Performance Process Cycle

Every game is composed of two parts: an outer game and an inner game. The outer game is played against an external opponent to overcome external obstacles and reach an external goal. The inner game is the game that takes place in the mind of the player and is played to overcome all habits of mind that inhibit excellence in performance.

Timothy Gallwey, author of The Inner Game of Tennis

IN THIS CHAPTER I introduce the core model that runs throughout this book: the Performance Process Cycle. This model explores the experiences traders go through as they play the outer game versus the market and the inner game against themselves.

THE PERFORMANCE PROCESS CYCLE

The Performance Process Cycle seeks to capture the different experiences traders face as they move through the trading process. It looks at the interplay between the two games, the inner game and the outer game, and how this manifests in people's mental game.

The model is a very simple way of exploring something that is inherently complex. It is a roadmap to help manage the interplay between your self and your ego – one that allows you to navigate your way through trades and trading decisions.

The model is comprised of four quadrants, each representing a crucial stage in the trading process. Two of these stages place greater emphasis on psychological management of one's self – focusing on managing one's state of mind and adopting appropriate psychological stances when trading. The other two stages are more transactional and prioritise physical and cognitive engagement when dealing with markets, risks, and uncertainty.

This chapter offers a quick and basic introduction to the Performance Process Cycle. The cycle will be explored in greater detail as we progress through the book.

Figure 1 shows the basic Performance Process Cycle.

Figure 1: The 'basic' Performance Process Cycle

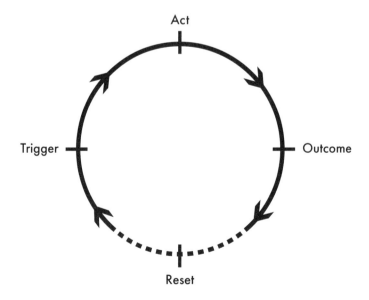

The cycle commences at the 'Reset' and moves clockwise through the 'Trigger', 'Act' and 'Outcome' events, before returning to the Reset and starting another cycle.

The cycle line is a boundary between the trader's internal world (within the circle) and their external world (everything outside of it). Here the two worlds and the trader's two games come into contact.

The trader's internal world is their self. Their external world consists of the markets they engage with and the key stakeholders in their world, such as family, close friends, colleagues and – if they are employed – the organisation they work for. It also includes broader environmental influences.

THE CONTACT BOUNDARY BETWEEN THE TRADER'S INTERNAL AND EXTERNAL WORLDS

The trader's process is inextricably tied to the contact point where their internal and external worlds meet. This is where they receive new data, news or instructions from the outside world, before evaluating and considering it within their own internal world. Ultimately, this information is used to inform the decisions and actions they take within their trading process.

Information crosses this contact boundary continually. This exchange of information impacts and shapes the trader's internal world, who they are, how they act, and what they do, which they then project back out to their external world, helping to incrementally shape it.

This ongoing exchange of information is reflexive in nature, impacting people and shaping their world. This process, replicated across millions of people's contact boundaries, shapes the markets, and contributes to their movements, seeding both chaos and order in the markets.

Figure 2 highlights the Performance Process Cycle, emphasising the trader's internal and external worlds and the information flow across the contact boundary.

Figure 2: The Performance Process Cycle and the trader's internal and external worlds

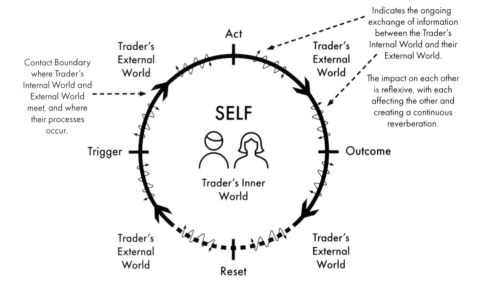

THE FOUR QUADRANTS

The cycle comprises four quadrants, with transitions to new quadrants occurring at each of the four cardinal compass points – north, south, east and west.

The progression through the stages and transitions is a continual and recurring process, like all cycles. Traders will often have several simultaneous cycles occurring, maybe representing multiple trades; but for the purpose of clarity, we will concentrate on a single cycle.

Traders will often have higher- and lower-level cycles occurring too, since this is a fractal process. As an example, managing a portfolio may be occurring at the higher process cycle level, with hedging and micro-trade management occurring at lower-level cycles. The major cycle is dominant, influencing the trader's actions on the lower-level cycles, and the actions on the lower-level cycles are likely to impact the higher-level cycle.

In order to minimise complexity and to honour an important principle of mine, this book will take a 'less is more' attitude and keep talk of higher- and lower-level cycles to a minimum throughout this book, while acknowledging that everyone will have them playing out in some way.

Each circuit of the cycle should commence with the trader checking-in – acknowledging their purpose – at the Reset. As they navigate their way around the circle, all actions should be executed in alignment with this purpose.

THE FIRST QUADRANT: THE BEING PHASE

The first quadrant of the cycle – between the Reset and Trigger transitions – is the 'Being Phase'. It is also the first of the two 'Power Zones'.

The Being Phase is where the trader prepares and primes themselves for the coming trading process. The Being Phase energises and gives power to the trader as they prepare for a circuit of the cycle. At this point the trader should be focused on being in an optimal state for the challenge ahead and adopting an appropriate stance (way of being), for the upcoming process. By doing this the trader charges their 'mental capital', ready to be used to achieve their purpose.

Mental capital describes the energy that powers a person's cognitive and emotional capabilities. It enables a trader to think clearly, make sense of situations, decide and act optimally, self-manage, and remain resilient and resolute.

Under pressure, and even over the course of a day, people's mental capital depletes – though it can be rationed and partially replenished. The trader's mental capital is a precious and finite resource that must be carefully managed.

I term this area a 'Power Zone', as the actions of a trader here empower them and give them an advantage in the upcoming trading process. Failing to engage effectively with the Being Phase undermines the trader's process before it even begins. This also distinguishes the quadrant from the more transactional nature of the second and third quadrants.

Figure 3: The Performance Process Cycle – Quadrant 1: the Being Phase

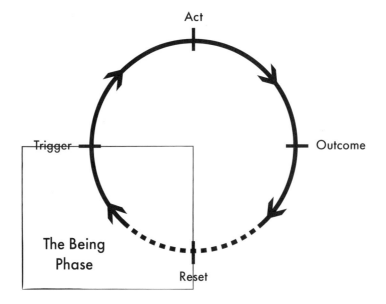

THE SECOND QUADRANT: THE PRODUCTION PHASE

From the Being Phase, a Trigger event occurs that takes the trader into the 'Production Phase' (The first Activity Zone). Traders need a reason to act, and that reason often comes from a Trigger event. This can originate from different sources, such as a piece of breaking news, a game-changing data point, insightful research or analyst's reports, or a thought-provoking opinion piece. Alternatively, the Trigger can arise from a trader's own analysis of the market and related events. In the context of portfolio management, Triggers may also stem from the need to rebalance, adjust, or hedge a portfolio or risk. Similarly, traders may receive instructions from clients, managers, or stakeholders that trigger their decision-making process. There could also be signals which trigger traders' actions, perhaps a break of a key level, some technical analysis indicator, a read of the market sentiment, a perceived shift in market liquidity, a system buy or sell signal or a need to fulfil a client order.

Once the Trigger occurs, the trader enters a process of 'sense-making', which leads to a process of narrative formation, updating or modification of existing narratives, new idea generation. Depending on the context this could be a rapid and near automated process of seconds, or even micro-seconds, or a much longer process lasting anywhere from hours to days or even weeks.

With the narrative formed or updated, the trader then has to decide whether to place a trade and how. This part of the process is defined by the trader's purpose and laid out in their *playbook* – a combination of the strategies, tactics, rules, and guidelines they intend to use in their process. Think of it as the system they use or the method they apply. Most traders do not have a *written* or clearly defined playbook, often it is implied by the system or method they are using, or the behaviours they repeatedly practice.

Assuming the trader has prepared well during the Being Phase, they should have good reserves of mental capital to help them find trades, assess them, then decide how best to place them.

Figure 4: The Performance Process Cycle – Quadrant 2: the Production Phase

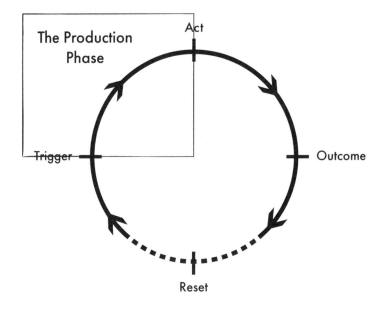

THE THIRD QUADRANT: THE PERFORMANCE PHASE

In transitioning from the Production Phase to the Performance Phase of the cycle (also known as Activity Zone 2) the trader crosses over to the right-hand side of the circle (see Figure 5). The transitioning event is an action they do or a decision they make. Since many decisions do not involve an action, the decision not to act is considered an act for the purpose of this book. It has repercussions.

This is where the trader is at risk – in the face of the radical uncertainty of markets. This is also where the *performance* occurs. Trading is a performance activity, not a transactional one. Their decision, whatever it was, bears their name and thus they are exposed to the decisions they made. This is where their ego is more likely to become a factor in the process, as it seeks to steer its host towards acting in ways that win the admiration of his or her peers. Whether the trader is working alone, independently or in a group, the ego overlooks the presence or absence of peers, and acts as if peers are present and aware of the trader's actions.

The performance phase is undoubtedly the most emotionally-charged period for traders, as a myriad of factors come into play. From fluctuations in the ever-changing markets and price volatility, to the uncertainty of the outcome and personal risk involved, traders experience an influx of heightened emotions. Additionally, the weight of expectations that they place on themselves further compounds these emotions, creating a highly charged and potentially challenging environment to navigate.

A trader who can maintain an optimal state throughout the Performance Phase will be more likely to stick to their process and less likely to fall victim to the self-sabotaging, dark side of the ego. They will retain their 'mental fortitude', which helps them preserve their precious mental capital

Mental fortitude is the key to emotional mastery during the Performance Phase. It is what keeps a trader in control and on-process under incredible pressure. Few, if any, traders survive this phase completely unscathed and without some depletion of mental capital.

Figure 5: The Performance Process Cycle – Quadrant 3: the Performance Phase

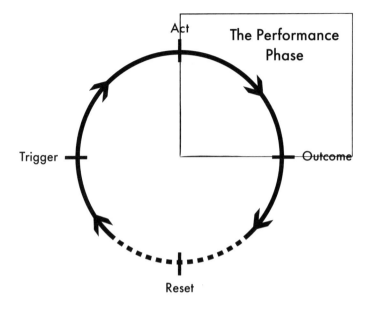

THE FOURTH QUADRANT: THE LETTING GO PHASE

The Letting Go Phase focuses on how the trader mentally disengages from the outcome of a trade.

During the Performance Phase, individuals experience a wide array of emotions, ranging from fist-pumping positivity to extreme negativity and despair. This emotional rollercoaster disrupts objective decision-making and rational assessments of situations. No one is immune to this. We are all human, we are all wired the same way. Strong feelings get generated, and they can be hard to simply dismiss.

The trade reaches its conclusion with the outcome of the trader's decisions. For the sake of simplicity, most descriptions in this book will refer to closed trades, but it is helpful to acknowledge that Letting Go refers to open and ongoing situations too, where the perceived outcome or current value of the trade is negative, even though the actual outcome has not yet been realised. This is particularly the case for traders (and investors) running long-term and complex portfolios, relative value or long-short trading risk, strategic directional trades, trend following systems, and other similar type trading strategies.

For a trader to truly and fully let go, they need to achieve both physical and mental closure. These two rarely occur together, particularly when the trader's ego becomes attached to the trade, and their emotions are elevated.

Traders who manage to maintain an optimal trading state up to this point and have retained their mental fortitude are more likely and better able to get mental closure, accept the outcome of what happened – to let go – and then move on through to the Reset.

By this stage of the cycle, the trader's mental capital has nonetheless depleted by varying degrees. The exception is where a trader achieves a rare 'flow state'. A flow state, also called 'being in the zone' is when someone is fully focused, energised and deeply engaged in an activity. It brings a sense of timelessness, heightened awareness, and lack of self-consciousness. Flow is linked to increased creativity, productivity and performance, and tends not to see energy levels deplete.

The ability to let go is the greatest and most under-appreciated skill a trader can possess. Once a trader lets go, they can pass through the Reset and return to the Being Phase. There they can restore balance and replenish their mental capital, ready for the next circuit of the cycle.

It is in the Letting Go Phase, more than anywhere else, that the mental game is mastered and won.

Figure 6: The Performance Process Cycle – Quadrant 4: the The Letting Go Phase

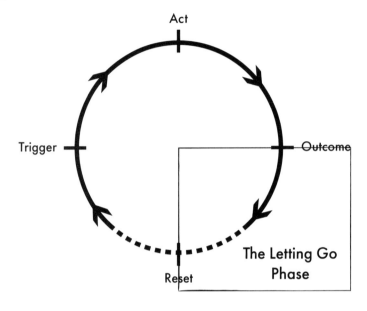

RADICAL UNCERTAINTY AND THE TRADER'S DEATH SPIRAL

'Radical uncertainty' is a phrase used to describe situations where cause and effect are impossible to discern and resolve in real time. Markets *always* exist in states of radical uncertainty, even when they appear calm and supposedly predictable.

However, the consequences of radical uncertainty are primarily felt during times of heightened emotion on the right side of the cycle. When it comes to assessing outcomes, the ego operates in a binary manner, seeking validation for its host. As a result, when confronted with unpredictable circumstances, it prioritises outcomes over process and tasks and may even hijack the trading process if a negative outcome is perceived.

Once the ego is in control, it can be difficult for the trader to get the mental closure they need. The ego does not care for Resetting and getting back to an optimal state of being. Once it has hijacked the process, it heads in the direction of achieving its own purpose of seeking acclaim. When this happens, it is difficult for the trader to attend to the needs of the task. Instead, they will find themselves attending to the needs of the ego.

As a result, the trader is unable to Reset. Now they start to short-circuit the cycle, jumping straight back to the Act, bypassing the Being Phase and the Production Phase.

Figure 7: Short-circuiting the Performance Process Cycle

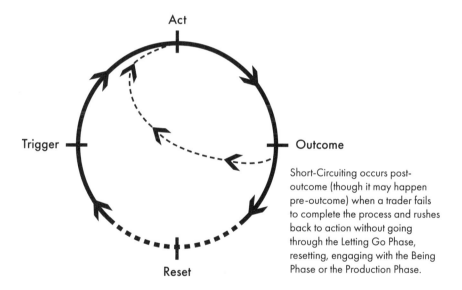

Short-Circuiting occurs post-outcome (though it may happen pre-outcome) when a trader fails to complete the process and rushes back to action without going through the Letting Go Phase, resetting, engaging with the Being Phase or the Production Phase.

Once this starts, the trader is off-process. They are now working towards an ego-driven purpose and are no longer present and attending to the primary needs of their task. A new, unproductive cycle commences where the trader starts to spiral.

Figure 8: The short-circuited performance process cycle

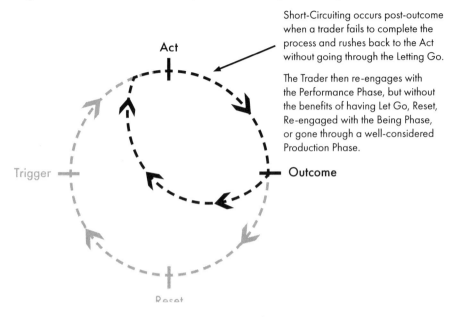

Short-Circuiting occurs post-outcome when a trader fails to complete the process and rushes back to the Act without going through the Letting Go.

The Trader then re-engages with the Performance Phase, but without the benefits of having Let Go, Reset, Re-engaged with the Being Phase, or gone through a well-considered Production Phase.

Act

Trigger

Outcome

Reset

Once a trader starts to embark on this new short-circuited process cycle, a fundamental shift occurs. Gradually, their process and actions become no longer entirely their own; rather, they become increasingly influenced by market forces and situational factors. The ego plays a crucial role in this transformation, serving as the conduit through which the market takes ownership of the trader's actions and approach.

Once this short-circuited cycle is in play, it can become a self-reinforcing unproductive cycle. This is because the trader's ego becomes increasingly dependent on the market as it takes over their decision-making. Given that the market is a crowd, the ego ends up conforming to the wants and demands of this crowd.

This self-reinforcing unproductive cycle now becomes a negative feedback loop, and the trader starts spiralling. That harms both the trader's effectiveness and their sense of self as they lose control of their actions.

Letting go becomes increasingly difficult as the trader lacks the clarity of mind, particularly as their mental capital depletes and their mental fortitude erodes. The spiralling process takes the trader deeper into this negative state. Unless they can exit this, they risk going into the Trader's Death Spiral. Here severe losses and underperformance become baked-in, and the trader's mental state and personal well-being deteriorate. Their ability to act rationally, let alone objectively, becomes increasingly compromised.

Figure 9 shows what results: the 'Trader's Death Spiral'.

Figure 9: Spiralling and the trader's death spiral

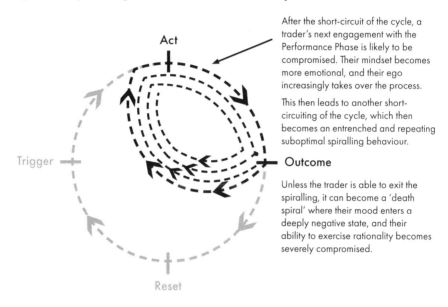

After the short-circuit of the cycle, a trader's next engagement with the Performance Phase is likely to be compromised. Their mindset becomes more emotional, and their ego increasingly takes over the process.

This then leads to another short-circuiting of the cycle, which then becomes an entrenched and repeating suboptimal spiralling behaviour.

Unless the trader is able to exit the spiralling, it can become a 'death spiral' where their mood enters a deeply negative state, and their ability to exercise rationality becomes severely compromised.

Every trader is susceptible to entering the death spiral. This is not a bug in our operating system; it is a feature of who we are. We see the same process in poker when players are said to be going into a tilt state. Poker players experiencing tilt enter a state where they begin to make unwise decisions and display poor judgement. As this state intensifies, their emotions become more heightened, which further hinders their ability to play effectively. Progressively the rational parts of their brain relinquish control, and the player becomes owned by the other players. Soon their money will start to become the other players'.

This is why the ability to let go is such a superpower. Only by letting go can you exit the spiralling behaviour and start to return to optimal process and performance. As we progress through the latter stages of this book, and delve more into the section on the Letting Go Phase, it will become clear how fundamental this is to great trading performance.

THE PERFORMANCE PROCESS CYCLE AS A WAVE

The Performance Process Cycle can also be expressed as a wave, whereby the upper half of the wave contains the Production and Performance phases where the trader more directly interacts with the market. The lower half encompasses the Being and Letting Go phases, referred to as the Power Zones, which honours the transformative impact that these phases have on trader's process and thus their performance.

Figure 10 shows one cycle, in the form of a single wave.

Figure 10: The Performance Process Cycle as a wave

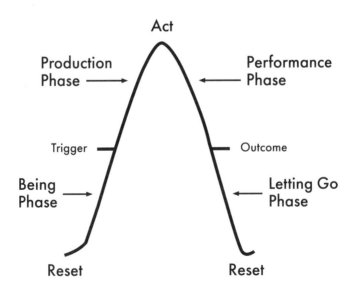

MULTIPLE WAVES

The wave format allows you to see the continuous nature of the Performance Process Cycle, whereby it can be viewed as a series of waves (see Figure 11), with each healthy completion of the cycle leading to the next wave.

Figure 11: The Performance Process Cycle as a series of waves

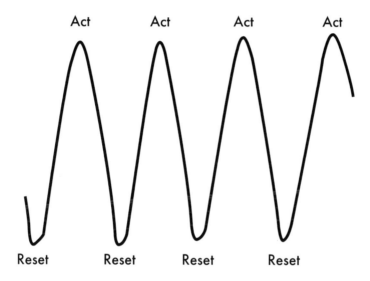

Figure 12 now shows what happens when a trader enters the death spiral when the Performance Process Cycle is shown in a wave format.

As the trader enters the spiralling action, their ability to control decisions gradually erodes. They are no longer resetting, and without the Reset they are unable to rest, replenish and rebalance. Their mental fortitude erodes, and their mental capital depletes.

Figure 12: The Performance Process Cycle as a series of waves with spiralling

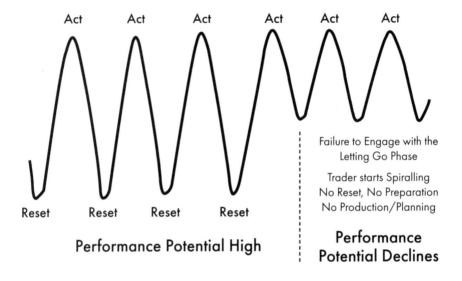

As they spiral, the trader is not engaging with the Power Zones but is trapped within the Activity Zones, and they are unable to reset and return to a balanced equilibrium. Their ego has taken control of their trading, their actions are increasingly owned by the market and their emotions will remain elevated. As this persists, their mental capital declines, then their performance potential declines, which is usually followed by an eventual loss of financial capital.

The Performance Process Cycle highlights a crucial concept mentioned earlier in this chapter: the inherent struggle between two games – one with the market, the outer game, and the other with one's self, which centres on the ego. The contact boundary where these two games meet is where you play your mental game and where you execute your process. Your process is like a golden chariot which can carry you through as you meet these two opposing forces, both of which are trying their best to throw you out of that chariot, one so the market wins and the other so that your ego takes the reins. You must try your damnedest, at all times and all stages of your work, to stay on-process and in that golden chariot. And when you do get thrown off it when faced with setbacks or distractions, it's crucial to do everything possible to get back on it. Because at the end of the day that golden chariot, which represents your process, is your only chance.

In the next chapter, I will introduce another key concept used in this book, that of 'behavioural slippage', which refers to the financial losses incurred, or potential profits foregone, by traders due to deviations from optimal processes and behaviours driven by their psychological tendencies.

CHAPTER 3

The Behavioural Gap

Every trader has to run their own race. No one else is going to run it for you.

Tom Dante, private trader known as 'Trader Dante'

AS A SEASONED trader, Kyle had amassed an impressive 23-year career in banking and hedge funds prior to landing his latest role as a senior trader at a prominent hedge fund.

His expertise in trading discretionary global macro, a trading strategy that involves using experience to make decisions based on analysing interest rates, currency movements and geopolitical events, had earned him a strong reputation in the industry. However, in this new role, Kyle was feeling the weight of high expectations and intense pressure to deliver results.

In his most recent role, he had suffered a setback when his own hedge fund venture ended in failure. Keen to restore his reputation, which he felt had taken a hit from the failure, he wanted to hit the ground running in his new role.

However, his first year at the new firm saw mediocre performance. His returns were not what they should have been in what was a very good year for the kind of strategy he employed.

By contrast, Syed was a young retail trader in his third year of trading.

He was based in India and came from a middle-class family. His father had bankrolled him, and he was desperate to succeed and repay his father's faith. Syed had been on several courses, had learned a couple of trading systems and had studied the approaches of some well-known traders in the Indian stock market.

Having blown up his first two accounts, Syed was now on his third account. Some of the people he had learned trading from were producing reasonable returns in a challenging year, and Syed was now piling the pressure on himself.

Both these traders, at opposite ends of the trading experience spectrum, were in a similar battle with themselves.

In Kyle's case, impacted by his recent failure, his ego was interfering far too much. For Syed, still early in his trading career, the problem was he had not yet given his self the chance to learn and develop the abilities needed to succeed. Inspired by his ego, he put so much pressure on himself that he had become unable to learn.

Both traders approached me and provided a list of behaviours they wanted to fix. These included:

- Overtrading
- Oversizing
- Undersizing
- Grabbing profits
- Running losses
- Hesitating through self-doubt
- Taking trades through fear of missing out (FOMO)
- Micromanaging their positions
- Not allowing their trades to play out
- Looking to prove themselves right
- Allowing themselves to be influenced by the views of others

- Lack of discipline

- Impatience

- Regret trading

- Boredom trading

- Seeking perfection on entry

- Not taking profits when they had hit their target

- Moving stops

It does not matter whether you have been trading for three years or 23 years, you are fallible to these sorts of behaviours. They are all elements of 'behavioural slippage', a term which describes the difference between what a trader *could* achieve if they were able to adhere to a good process which has a positive expectancy (an edge) and what they actually *do* achieve. Behavioural interference factors reduce their edge.

If the trader's potential performance is high – as was the case with Kyle, the experienced trader – they may still produce a positive return, but it may be far lower than it could have been. This difference, caused by behavioural slippage, is the 'behavioural gap'.

Figure 13: Behavioural slippage

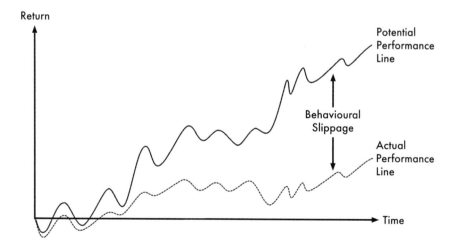

During periods where potential performance is much lower, possibly due to market conditions or a poorly performing system in an unfavourable market cycle, behavioural slippage contributes to the actual performance being negative, as shown in Figure 14. This compounds the pressure on a trader.

Figure 14: Behavioural slippage in low-performing traders

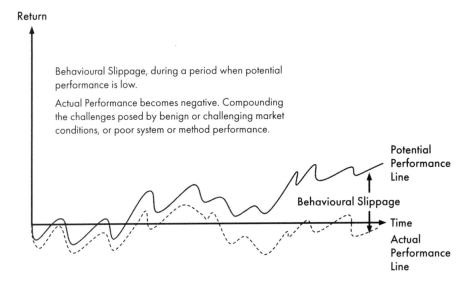

The concept of these behavioural slippage charts came to me when I was working with a client called Rowen.

Rowen had transitioned from a sell-side role at a bank to a buy-side position in a hedge fund. Sell-side roles are typically where traders act as market-makers, acting as an intermediary between buyers and sellers. Buy-side roles are where traders are given access to capital, often in a hedge fund, and they use that to trade in the markets on the firm's behalf.

Rowen had been working for three years at the fund but had consistently underperformed his expectations. He also felt he had made many strong market calls, but had failed to fully monetise these, leaving, as he described it, "serious money on the table."

Since moving to the hedge fund, Rowen had been writing detailed trading plans in his journal.

When he told me about this, I suggested he look back and assess how well his planned trades had performed in the market. This would allow him to establish the veracity of his ideas and to see if (and what) the failure to stick to his plans was really costing him.

It transpired that there was a huge difference between the returns he would have made had he followed his plans and his actual performance.

During the three-year period he looked at, his actual returns averaged around 4%, but the theoretical returns were on average close to 45%.

It was unrealistic for Rowen to have performed to the full potential highlighted by his assessment of his trades. Nonetheless, the degree of behavioural slippage was huge. There was significant room for him to close that gap. Even a small improvement would lead to far better returns.

When we delved into his performance, he mentioned experiencing many of the damaging behaviours that Kyle and Syed had detailed.

BEHAVIOURS AS SYMPTOMS

Like Kyle and Syed, Rowen wanted to fix these behaviours. But the behaviours themselves were not the problem: they were merely manifestations of something else.

Taking profit too quickly, running losses too far, panicking, hesitating, getting sucked in by FOMO, lacking discipline, impatience; all of these and more are ingredients in the cocktail of trader behaviours that make – and are a factor of working in – conditions of radical uncertainty. All traders exhibit some combination of these behaviours.

Think of these as unforced errors, similar to those found in tennis. Even the best players miss a few sitters, double fault a few times, hit an easy overhead smash long, or place an easy volley into the net. These errors don't always indicate a lack of skill, perfection is impossible, but when they happen with too much repetition, they may flag that there are other, sometimes deeper issues, at work.

A key issue at play for Rowen was that he had failed to successfully adjust from his sell-side role to a new buy-side one. He was now trading without the security that came from having significant flow income behind him.

The adjustment from sell-side to buy-side is a huge one to make, far more difficult than many traders realise. Rowen's ego was not trusting his self to work in this different way. As a result, his anxiety levels were often elevated, which led to him failing to trust his ideas, which were actually very strong. This lack of trust in his self, often at key moments, contributed to persistent sub-optimal trading performance.

Coming back to the two traders featured at the start of this chapter.

In Kyle's case, he desperately wanted to prove to himself and others that his failure was a blip. As a result, he had adopted a 'win at all costs' mentally. That cost was the corruption of his process, which was contributing to sub-optimal performance. The behaviours he described, notably oversizing, were symptoms of that corruption, and seemed to be the main source of his behavioural slippage. He was getting in the way of his own process.

In Syed's case, as a novice trader, he was so keen to achieve success so quickly that he was bypassing the learning process and trying to force success. While some simplistic systematic approaches can be learned quickly, trading is a highly skilled activity and for the most part cannot be learned and mastered in a few short months, and in most cases, even over a couple of years. Syed's ego was setting unrealistic expectations. The 'needs' of his ego stopped him from focusing on learning the game.

The primary focus of this book is on developing a strong inner game, but it's important to recognise that a strong inner game alone is not enough. Success in trading also requires a sound understanding of the outer game. If a trader is playing the outer game poorly, or is engaged in the wrong outer game altogether, it can have a negative impact on their inner game. In such cases, the trader's ego may react strongly, further compounding the problem.

When this happens, traders may become even more determined to make a failing outer game strategy work, leading to even greater stress and frustration. Therefore, it's crucial to strike a balance between developing a strong inner game and acquiring the skills and knowledge necessary to succeed in the outer game.

Rowen was aware that he had to adapt his outer game to better align with the realities of working on the buy-side. He knew this at the conscious level, but at the subconscious level his ego would not let him. Through my coaching sessions with Rowen, he was able to begin accepting his new and adapted behaviours. As a result, there was a marked improvement in his performance, which he has since continued to make progress on and has sustained over several years.

In subsequent years I have come to see how important the concept of behavioural slippage is. It can also be acquainted to the idea of a 'performance gap'. A performance gap is the difference between our actual performance and our potential.

My work with Rowen was also to prove formative in the development of a new framework, which I call 'The Two Risk Approaches'. This framework is foundational to the future discussions in this book, and it will be explored in greater detail in the next couple of chapters.

One final crucial point to consider on behavioural slippage. Potential profits, that you identified as part of your process but which you failed to capture (as opposed to hindsight calls), do not show up visibly in your P&L, but they do contribute to sub-optimal performance. However, these missed profits do hit your bottom line, thus showing up implicitly in your results. It can be hugely useful to track and monitor performance of your method as much as your actual performance. It is very unlikely that you will ever fully monetise every call, such is human nature, but if your process is significantly profitable and has a strong edge, that should provide a powerful incentive for traders to take steps to try to close their performance gap.

CHAPTER 4

The Two Risk Approaches – Player Approach Versus House Approach

In gambling, the many must lose in order that the few may win.

George Bernard Shaw, playwright

ONE PLEASANT MASSACHUSETTS evening in the spring of 1980, J.P. Massar was having dinner at a Chinese restaurant in Cambridge, the city known as 'Boston's Left Bank'. Cambridge is home to two of the world's leading academic institutions: Harvard University and Massachusetts Institute of Technology (MIT). Massar had studied computer science at the latter.

Massar overheard two men at a nearby table discussing the ins and outs of professional blackjack. Massar, a keen card player since his youth, had recently become fascinated by the game. He had heard it was possible to beat a casino using a technique known as card counting and tested out that claim on the powerful computer available to him at MIT.

Card counting is a technique used by blackjack players to try to gain an advantage over a casino. Players track the cards played, assigning a point value to every card, to help determine when the remaining cards in the deck shift the odds of winning – which are usually in the casino's favour – in the player's favour. Although not illegal, casinos usually expel and ban players who card count. A more detailed summary of the game of blackjack will be shown later in this chapter.

Massar had worked out that a team of players counting cards could signal to a team leader that a favourable setup was occurring at a blackjack table. The team leader could then place bets on that table strategically and win significantly more over time than they would lose. This led to Massar trying to develop and practise various card-counting techniques. However, thus far he had enjoyed relatively little success.

Intrigued by the conversation he overheard, Massar went over to introduce himself. One of the men was Bill Kaplan, a student at Harvard who had run a successful blackjack card-counting team in Las Vegas three years earlier.

Kaplan, who earned his BA at Harvard in 1977, had formed a team seeded with funds he had received by graduating as the university's outstanding scholar-athlete that year. Kaplan's card-counting team travelled to Las Vegas, where they managed to generate a return on his funds in excess of 3,500% in less than nine months.

Massar and Kaplan soon struck up a friendship, and Massar invited Kaplan to travel with him and some friends to Atlantic City. There, Kaplan observed the team, detailed what he thought were problems and then shared them with Massar.

What followed led to the formation of a new card-counting team that was to become the stuff of legends. Over the next two decades the team, formed of dozens of students from both MIT and Harvard rotated in and out over time, took on and beat many of the world's leading casinos. Their story was immortalised in Ben Mezrich's book, *Bringing Down the House*, which was later made into the movie *21*.

THE PLAYER APPROACH AND THE HOUSE APPROACH

There is much in the story of the card-counting team that can be applied to the trading themes discussed in this book.

Massar and Kaplan's outer game – the approach they took to engaging with their external opponent – required them to employ a card counting strategy to beat the casino's edge. The casino's outer game, by contrast, required them to take on their clients using a systematic style of playing which enabled them to monetise that marginal edge.

There are numerous different styles of outer game that traders and investors play, but all of them are equivalent in some way to either Massar and Kaplan's outer game or the casino's outer game.

A blackjack trading analogy is a simple way to introduce these two approaches. For those not familiar with blackjack, here is a short summary of the game's main features:

For this summary, and the analogy used in this book, I am referring to blackjack as played in a physical casino, rather than an online casino.

BLACKJACK SUMMARY

- The game is played with a standard deck of 52 cards. In casinos multiple decks, usually six to eight decks, are used at the same time.

- Each card has a point value: cards numbered from two to ten are worth their face value, while face cards (jack, queen and king) are worth ten points each, and aces are worth either one or 11 points (depending on which value would benefit the player the most).

- The goal of the game is to have a hand with a total value of 21 or as close to it as possible without going over.

- The game begins with the dealer dealing two cards to the player and two to themselves. One of the dealer's cards is face down (the hole card) and one is face up (the up card).

- Based on their own two cards, the player must then decide whether to 'hit' (ask for another card) or 'stand' (not take any more cards).

- If the player's hand goes over 21, they bust and lose the game automatically. (This clearly favours the dealer, who can win a game without even having to play.)

- Once the player stands, the dealer reveals their hole card and hits until they reach a total of 17 or higher.

- If the dealer busts, the player wins. If the player's hand is closer to 21 than the dealer's hand or the dealer busts, the player wins.

- If the player's hand and the dealer's hand have the same value, it is a 'push' and the player neither wins nor loses the game.

- Players have the option to double down (double the bet in exchange for receiving only one more card) or split their hand (if they have a pair) under certain circumstances.

- Blackjack (an ace and a ten-value card) is the best possible hand and pays out higher than a regular win.

- Any player who has a higher count than the dealer gets paid out an amount equivalent to their bet.

- All cards are collected and taken out of play before the next hand is dealt.

- The casino's edge in blackjack exists because when players bust, the dealer doesn't have to play their hand. Marginal as that edge is, it typically produces a house edge considered to be anywhere from 0.5% to 2.0%.

- There are slight variations in games and rules across different casinos and jurisdictions.

THE BLACKJACK TRADING ANALOGY

It is common for people who do not understand trading to say that it is just gambling, and the markets are merely a giant casino. In reality, casinos themselves are a market, in this case a physical marketplace for players where they are offered a variety of games to play.

The players are either 'gamblers' or 'gamers'. The distinction between these two terms is subtle but important. Gamblers are considered chancers who use the market to meet their needs for risk-taking, excitement and fun. Whereas gamers are engaging in the serious activity of playing, using skill and intelligence to find an edge and then earn a return – while doing something they enjoy.

Gamblers are not considered to have a clear and repeatable edge. They will win some and lose some. They may occasionally win big, as a consequence of the nature of randomness and luck, but if they keep playing, they will eventually lose. The exception is the odd lucky player who wins big then stops and does not play again.

Gamers are different. They either have an edge, or they seek to find one and learn how to apply it. For many gamers who know what their edge is, the challenge is being able to execute it with regularity and sustain it over time. J.P. Massar was a gamer, but during the early days of developing his system, before he met Kaplan, he was not able to make it work.

As we proceed through the book, I will still occasionally refer to the term casino, but increasingly casinos will be referred to as 'the house'. This is because they are the ones that set the rules and control the games. In other words, the casino is the owner of the house, and players are guests visiting it to try their luck.

Since the house sets the rules and controls the game, the game will be rigged in its favour, thus by default the house should always win in the long run, ensuring that it always comes out on top. This is the 'house's edge'.

In blackjack, the dealer at the table is the agent of the house; they play the game for the house against the players or groups of players. The players are playing for themselves against the house, they are the gamers and gamblers.

The typical setup of a game of blackjack appears as in Figure 15. Casinos typically have multiple blackjack tables operating at any one time.

Figure 15: The casino blackjack setup

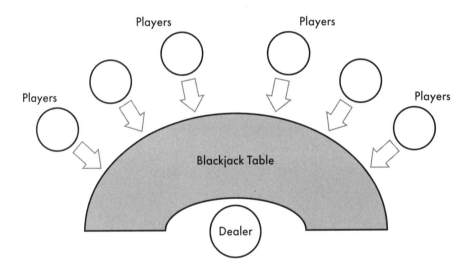

BLACKJACK:
THE HOUSE APPROACH

One of the features of blackjack is the 'house's edge'. Depending on what form of the game is being played, and by what rules, the house is deemed to have an approximate 2.0% edge over the average player, across all hands. Against experienced and skilled players, this edge is believed to diminish to as low as 0.5%.

Representing the house, the dealer must ensure they play using the system, method, or approach that the casino mandates. They will usually be allowed to exercise some small amount of discretion, but adherence to the casino's system is paramount.

By applying this system, the casino expects to win most of the time. It accepts it will lose occasionally, and that some of those losses may be outsized ones, but they expect to win many more small bets. With the edge in their favour, the casino assesses that the accumulation of small wins should add up to significantly more than the aggregate of the losses, including the fewer larger losses.

A population of bets for the house could look something like the 'win-loss tablet' in Figure 16. The size of losses are exaggerated, to emphasise a point.

Figure 16: Win-loss tablet: the house approach

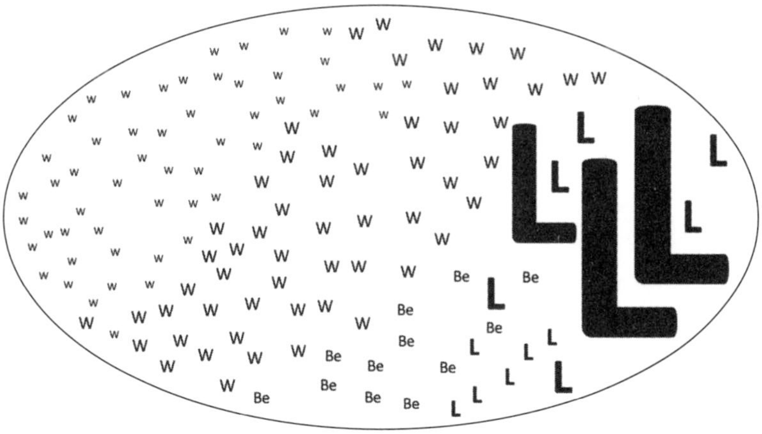

On this win-loss tablet, you will see mostly small or very small wins denoted by a 'W'. There are a few ties or break-evens denoted by 'Be' and some losses, with a few larger or very large losses denoted by an 'L'.

Over time this creates a return profile which produces a steady, though unspectacular move higher. While this appears to be all profit, a high fixed-cost base will take a considerable chunk out of this return.

Figure 17: A typical return profile for the house approach

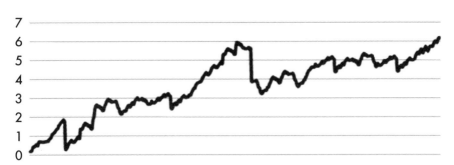

BLACKJACK:
THE PLAYER APPROACH

The player is playing against the house. They will use a range of techniques, skills and strategies to reduce the house's edge and take advantage of occasions when the statistical edge tips in their favour.

Skilled and experienced players use techniques such as card counting, shuffle tracking and hole carding, some of which are borderline in terms of legality. They also learn gameplay strategies that tip the edge towards them, though it never moves so far as to fully lean in their favour. The house still retains an edge, but it becomes increasingly marginal against skilled and experienced players.

For the sake of this analogy, I will not focus on the techniques mentioned above, but instead will focus exclusively on card counting.

At some point during the course of each game, the edge temporarily tips towards the players. Skilled card counters are able to recognise these moments, then adjust their betting strategy to play more aggressively and monetise when the edge is in their favour.

Casinos do not consider card counting to be an acceptable strategy. In their view, players who card count seek to gain an unfair advantage. They go to great lengths to identify such players and train their dealers in techniques that undermine the effectiveness of card counting.

Card counting itself is not difficult, but the ability to execute it continuously over many hours, without error and while appearing not to do it, is incredibly demanding. This challenge is complicated by the counter card-counting tactics undertaken by the house.

In blackjack a player must bet on every hand of cards in order to stay in the game, so even card-counting players must 'pay to play'. Since most of the time the odds are against the player, paying to play has a monetary cost even for the card counter. To lower this cost, players will keep bets small when the edge is clearly in the house's favour.

When a card-counting player assesses that the edge has moved in their direction, they act more aggressively by increasing their bet size. They must keep in mind that randomness remains a feature of the environment, and that the odds of them winning have only marginally increased. Hence, risk management principles in relation to bet size still apply.

The population of bets for a card-counting player over time may look something like Figure 18.

Figure 18: Win-loss tablet: the card-counting player approach

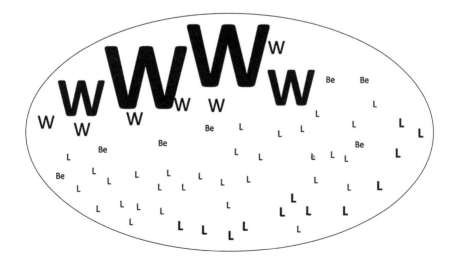

On this player's win-loss tablet, you see a relatively low proportion of large or very large wins, a few break-evens and many more losses than wins. However, larger losses are relatively few, and most losses are very small. The accumulated sum of the wins will ideally be larger than the accumulated sum of the losses. Sizes on this win-loss tablet are again exaggerated for emphasis.

You will notice that the population of bets on the player's win-loss tablet is much sparser than the house's example. This is to emphasise that the player is far more sporadic in their gameplay. The house has to play all the time, whenever there is a customer or client demand, while any player can choose when to play and can walk away whenever they want.

The return profile of a player over time might look something like Figure 19. Long periods of steady drawdown, or bleed, are punctuated by occasional and sometimes spectacular gains.

Figure 19: A typical return profile for the player approach

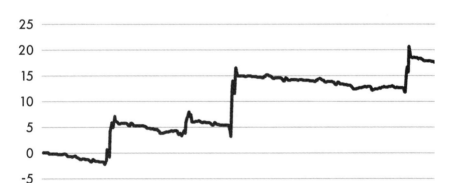

This understanding of the dynamics of blackjack lays the groundwork for the next chapter, in which we will see how these lessons can be applied to the world of trading.

CHAPTER 5

The Two Risk Approaches and Trading

The truth is that the BEST LOSER is the long-term winner.

Art Simpson, author of Phantom of the Pits

I N FALL OF 1992 three hedge fund traders sat in a dimly lit office in New York discussing the foreign exchange (FX) markets. They had been focusing in on the discord between the government of the United Kingdom and the chiefs of Germany's central bank, the Bundesbank.

The UK economy was in a deep recession and the country's leaders wanted to cut interest rates to ease the pressure on people and businesses. The UK government was, however, restricted from being able to cut rates without the approval of its European partner countries in the European Rate Mechanism (ERM).

The UK's membership of the ERM required it to maintain the British Pound's (GBP) value against the German Deutsche Mark (DEM). If the UK had cut rates at that time, it would almost certainly have led to the GBP dropping against the DEM below the lower boundary the UK had agreed to maintain.

The Bundesbank, for their part, had been running a regime of high interest rates in the wake of the reunification of East and West Germany. The purpose of this was to put a lid on any inflationary pressures which may result from reunification. But this policy was forcing the UK to keep interest rates far higher than the UK government felt was warranted by their own economic situation.

The three traders in the office discussed this at length, then one of them suggested their belief that there was a 95% likelihood that the British would lose this argument with the Germans. As a result, they would withdraw from the ERM, which would lead to a sharp drop in the value of the GBP.

The trader who suggested this was Stanley Druckenmiller. The fund was Soros's Quantum Fund. In the conversation with him were George Soros, the head of the fund, and the fund's currency specialist, Robert Johnson

Druckenmiller believed that the potential profit to be made from this situation was so obvious that they should commit 100% of the firm's capital to shorting GBP, then buying it back lower after its value had dropped, thus realising a significant profit. Soros wanted him to go further, placing as much as 200% of the firm's capital on the trade.

On 16 September 1992 the UK government announced it was withdrawing from the ERM. GBP plummeted in value, dropping 10% versus the DEM. In the end, the events unfolded so quickly that the fund was not able to get their full size on, but they did manage to allocate around 150% of the firm's capital, and Soros's fund earned over £1 billion profit that day alone.

THE PLAYER APPROACH
TO TRADING

Soros, Druckenmiller and Johnson took on the house – the Bank of England on this occasion – and beat it convincingly.

Theirs was a classic player-approach trade. Though they committed a significant size capital to the trade, around one and a half times the fund's capital, had the trade not worked out their loss would have been small compared to the potential profit, and according to Soros, no more than 4% of the firm's capital.*

Their approach was akin to the card-counting strategy used in blackjack. They had identified a trade setup, and they deemed the edge had tipped towards them – with a very favourable risk-to-reward ratio. This meant that if they were right, their profit would be several multiples of what they would lose if wrong.

In contrast to the blackjack trading analogy, their understanding of their edge was based on a subjective assessment of probability, rather than the objective assessment which is possible when a player is counting cards. Nonetheless, the principles were the same.

Player approaches usually require traders to use a form of subjective analysis, whereby they assess the risk-reward and trade if they deem the possible return is sufficient compensation for a low win rate.

---

* This is a video clip which described their risk on the trade: George Soros & Stanley Druckenmiller on breaking the Bank of England (1993), www.youtube.com/watch?v=4DYnzBfHYAQ.

THE HOUSE APPROACH
TO TRADING

Though Soros and his colleagues used the player approach in their trade, much earlier in Soros's career he preferred to implement a house approach, even though he was on the player side of the table.

Soros had started out as a financial analyst. During the 1950s and 1960s he worked for investment firms in London and New York, and noticed that there were significant price differences in the valuations of near-identical financial assets in different locations across global markets.

These differences offered the potential for arbitrage. Arbitrage occurs when traders simultaneously buy and sell near-identical securities, currencies or commodities in different markets in order to take advantage of marginal differences in price. The risk on these trades is considered very low, though they have to be done in large sizes to make them viable, which creates a different type of risk which only becomes apparent when liquidity starts to dry-up.

The disparity in prices, which Soros observed, existed because of global capital controls. These capital controls made arbitrating across different countries nearly impossible. But Soros, not one to be easily put off by a challenge, found innovative ways to get around these controls. He soon started making significant profits, initially for his employers and then for wealthy individuals who invested their capital with him.

The commissions he took from the large gains he made for his investors were to be the source of his initial wealth. This activity later gave rise to the creation of his hedge fund businesses, where he was able to put more capital to work and use leverage to increase the size of the risks.

This type of trading is considered akin to the approach used by the house, hence the term 'house approach'. In the gambling world, the house is the term for the casino, but applying it in markets, it stands for those who provide liquidity to markets. This includes providers of liquidity such as market-makers, regional and investment banks, central banks, exchanges and physical energy and commodity traders (collectively known as the sell-side). The traders in these firms are agents of the house seeking to take advantage of the house's edge. Their provision of liquidity and pricing to the market makes it possible for clients and customers to participate in it. The house approach often requires these traders to work collectively in systematic or semi-systematic ways, though with some discretion.

Sell-side firms traditionally make money on these activities by charging fees or margins for market access and warehousing the risk and transactions that pass through their books, rather than assuming risk. They will often hold short-term risks to take advantage of their proximity to the market liquidity, though more sophisticated liquidity providers may hold significant longer-term risks at times.

The buy-side (hedge funds, family offices, proprietary trading firms and internal proprietary trading desks inside sell-side firms), are the players who step up to the table, though many firms, and traders within them, may be using house approaches.

As with Soros and his arbitrage transactions, many of the traders using house-approach strategies in buy-side roles do so to take advantage of market anomalies. Buy-side traders exploit these using pricing models, arbitrage structures and mean-reversion trading approaches. Jim Simons, considered to be one of the most successful traders of the last 30 years, has leveraged the house approach at his renowned Medallion Fund as a buy-side trader.

The pure house-approach trader is largely indifferent to long-term market direction; whichever way the market heads, they extract value from it. Though many directional traders do so while working principally with a house-approach strategy.

Many small retail traders are also engaged in house-approach-style trades. Though they consider themselves to be players, their activities (trying to scalp ticks or pips from the market) add to the liquidity of the market. Like the floor traders from which they are descended, they provide liquidity to the exchanges (the house) while being individual players.

I hope that was not too confusing. If it was, stay with me; it will come to you.

In the next chapter we will look at the implications of these two approaches for the trader, in terms of how they engage with markets, how they take and manage risk, and their different psychological impacts.

CHAPTER 6

The Two Approaches and the Trader's Psychological Contract

The first rule of trading – there are probably many first rules – is don't get caught in a situation in which you can lose a great deal of money for reasons you don't understand.

Bruce Kovner, legendary trader featured in Market Wizards[1]

YUMIKO WAS AN FX trader working at a London bank. During a coaching session she shared with me the details of a trade she had taken in the summer of 2014 and the frustration it caused her.

Yumiko had mentioned to her colleagues that she was bullish on the US dollar-Japanese yen exchange rate, USDJPY, and believed it could head higher, from 102 to 120 yen to the dollar, in the second half of the year. She decided to back her call, and in July she bought $25m USDJPY at 102.

She held the position for a few weeks, the longest she had ever run a trade. By early September it had started moving in the right direction, hitting 105.

Although Yumiko was in profit over $700,000 on the trade, her natural inclination was to actively trade in and out around volatile markets events. She was a classic house-approach spot FX trader; running positions for long periods was not her forte.

Ahead of that month's US non-farm payroll data's release, she decided to book the profit she had on the USDJPY at 105.

With volatility increasing after the release of the non-farm payroll data, the USDJPY started trending higher. Yumiko was now frustrated that she had booked her profit rather than sitting with the trade.

As it moved higher still, she decided to fight this rally, which contradicted the long-term view she had expressed. She initially shorted USDJPY at 107. Within a couple of days it was trading at 108, Yumiko cut the short.

Her attempts to short continued over the next few weeks, sometimes getting the timing right but mostly losing money. Often, she would sell a rally then be forced to buy it back higher. She never reinstated the long trade.

USDJPY hit 120 in December.

Had Yumiko stayed with the trade plan she would have made over $3.5m on the trade. Instead, with all the failed attempts to trade around it, she had lost money. Worse still was the damage it did to her mindset, which caused her to cannibalise her normal trading approach and thus pass up many other short-term trading opportunities.

With reference to the blackjack analogy, Yumiko had been caught trying to play both sides of the table at the same time. She was caught between the two approaches. She was trying to trade for the longer term using a player approach but was locked into the mindset, behaviours and actions of the house approach which she was more used to, and highly skilled at.

Hybridising the two approaches can be done, and to a degree is often done by traders to some degree, but one approach is usually dominant, and becomes the main focus of a trader's approach.

Because the two approaches are so contradictory to each other it takes a highly skilled, experienced and disciplined trader – one with an understanding of how and when to play both sides of the table – to be able to play both approaches together, and even then, it is incredibly rare.

To emphasise this, look at the following two statements: which one do you feel is correct?

You never go broke taking a profit.

You never go broke taking a loss.

This question resides at the very heart of the risk philosophy of the two approaches.

There is no definitive right or wrong answer to this question. But for every trader there is an appropriate answer that will depend on which approach to trading they use.

Traders who take a pure house approach will often live by the mantra that 'You never go broke taking a profit'. When I worked in a bank as a market-maker, this was the dominant philosophy. It is also the philosophy of the house or casino. They take many small profits and accumulate these, which then compensate for the occasional larger losses which come along periodically, as demonstrated in the win-loss tablet for the house shown earlier in Figure 16.

Traders who take a pure player approach believe that 'You never go broke taking a loss', though the caveat here is that losses are limited in size. This way the trader takes many relatively small losses, which are compensated for by the outsize wins which come along periodically based on their method. This philosophy is akin to the card counter's approach, as demonstrated in the win-loss tablet for the player shown earlier in Figure 18.

These two philosophies, when applied to trading, create two very different approaches to taking risk, different approaches to identifying opportunities and value, different risk management frameworks, and a personal psychology that is most optimal for the trading approach. These may at times even be contradictory to each other, and this can cause great confusion for the trader. As Yumiko found out to her cost.

It might be fair to say that really trading is not one, but two activities, one involves taking a player approach to taking and managing risk. The other is adopting a house approach. Each of the approaches requires a slightly different psychological contract the player makes with their self.

THE TRADER'S PSYCHOLOGICAL CONTRACT WITH THEIR SELF

A psychological contract is an implicit bargain, much like a contract of employment. It describes the nature of the relationship between you (an employer) and your inner self (the employee), and both parties' expectations and obligations.

Traders are one-person businesses. When it comes to what they do in their trading, the quality of their relationship with their self is the key to success. Therefore, the trader must create a psychological contract with their self.

Whichever trading approach you use, there is a bargain to be struck with your self so that you are aligned towards the same purpose. If you are not able to apply your self correctly in your approach, you may end up like Yumiko, caught between the two approaches.

THE PLAYER-APPROACH BARGAIN

Most traders start by using a house approach. Basic house approaches are simpler and can be used when traders are less skilled or experienced. In theory, house approaches tend to yield a positive return, making them psychologically easier to live with.

Early in my trading career, as a trader working in banks, I used a house approach, both as a market-maker, and as a user of arbitrage methods. Later in my career I morphed into a pure proprietary trader, still inside banks, who applied a player approach. My style, as a proprietary trader, meant my profits would come from placing large risk-reward style trades.

Winning trades only came along occasionally, and relied on me identifying them as potential opportunities where I could adopt a more aggressive risk stance. I would engage in searching for and trying many trade setups in the process to find the better opportunities. When it was clear that the trades were not ones I would run with, I would exit them relatively quickly and often for quite minimal losses. This philosophy was characterised by the above statement 'you never go broke taking a loss.'

The player approach, which I was using, could be psychologically taxing due to the erratic nature of profits, and prolonged periods where few opportunities were occurring and P&L would bleed away in a run of many losing trades, which though small would add up.

There was also added pressure of observing others outperforming, particularly colleagues who are using the house approach, which tends to accumulate P&L. There is also the pressure to meet the expectations of stakeholders, who are often looking for a steady return and are rarely comfortable with the drawdowns and P&L bleed associated with the player approach. Think of the scene in the movie *The Big Short*, where Michael Burry is under pressure from an investor, as the short positions he placed on the housing market continue to move against him.

The way to help yourself manage through these times, and stay on-process, is to formulate and accept a psychological bargain with yourself, which you refer back to during these challenging periods.

The bargain the player-approach trader makes with themselves, is that they agree to accept periods of loss and underperformance, missed opportunities, erratic returns and heightened P&L volatility, in return for potential to make excessive returns over time. The trader agrees to use their risk and capital skilfully to optimise the upside, while being extremely careful to manage drawdowns and not overexpose their downside. Traders must manage their psychology extremely carefully, particularly during barren spells and long spells of performance bleed.

THE HOUSE-APPROACH BARGAIN

If you have taken my description to mean that the house-approach trader's job is easier, this is not the case. Basic house-approach styles and methods are simple inductions into trading, and are quicker to learn, but they come with their own psychological challenges. There is also a big difference between the novice house-approach trader, who uses a relatively simple approach, compared to the seasoned house-approach trader, who typically uses a highly complex and specialised approach.

The main reason the house approach tends to seem psychologically easier is that profits tend to be more consistent and regular. However, the yield on the house approach tends to be lower, relative to the amount of capital put at risk, which can force the trader to adopt much larger size risk more regularly, exposing them to huge potential downside, particularly on the rare occasions where markets dislocate and liquidity dries up.

It only takes one blow-out in the markets to bring down a house-approach trader, or a house-approach trading business. Many of the big blow-ups which make the front pages of the newspapers are caused by house-approach styles going wrong.

The blow-up of the major hedge fund LTCM in 1998 was a house-approach trade going wrong. Likewise, many large hedge fund and bank failures were house-approach trades going wrong.

The tale of Einer Aas, a brilliant Scandinavian energy trader, highlights this at the personal level. Aas had single-handedly become the biggest player in Nordic energy and power markets over a two-decade period. His success made him one of Norway's highest earners. In 2016 alone he was Norway's largest taxpayer. Then in the space of a few days in 2018, his world came tumbling down. A dislocation occurred in the relationship between the German and Nordic power prices. Aas was unable to meet his margins, declared in default and placed under administration. His portfolio was liquidated in one day.

House-approach traders' philosophy may be 'you never go broke taking a profit', which is reflected in their tendency to book profits quickly and regularly, but they can and do go broke when an outlier event occurs and they cannot meet their margin call. Another term used to describe the house approach, is 'picking-up pennies in front of a steam roller', which highlights the jeopardy faced.

The bargain the house-approach trader accepts is that this approach tends to feel psychologically easier as profits tend to be more consistent and regular. However, the relatively low yields require traders to take large volumes of trades and assume significant amounts of risk. This approach comes with high-intensity and pressure to take high-risk volumes which require a need to stay on top of the risk, with an understanding that unexpected events represent a potential risk of ruin.

The legendary and brilliant house-approach trader Jesse Livermore said, "Trading is not a game for the stupid, the mentally lazy, the person of inferior emotional balance, or the get-rich-quick adventurer. They will die poor." Sadly, he died poor, by his own hand.

Some readers may question whether it is appropriate to use the adjective 'brilliant' to describe traders like Einer Aas or Jesse Livermore, who ultimately failed. However, I believe that their exceptional level of performance in taking risks warrants such a description. While they undoubtedly recognised that risk comes at a cost, they still displayed remarkable skill along the way.

In the case of house-approach traders such as Aas or Livermore, the risk often comes from extreme or outlier events hitting them when they have huge risk positions, and a subsequent loss of liquidity in the markets making it near impossible for them to exit. Player-approach traders' risk usually comes from their strategy no longer appearing to work or a continued bleed in their capital, which leads to them withdrawing from the market.

Aas's and Livermore's journeys demonstrated the essence of trading and the inherent risk involved.

THE HYBRID APPROACH

While many traders do in fact use hybrids of the two approaches, I have seen very few who have successfully been able to do this. And even in those cases, they have a clear bias towards using one method over the other. When they do use the other approach, it is usually for specific reasons, such as feeling out the market liquidity or taking advantage of special situations.

I sometimes used the house approach to probe the markets, but it was not the main approach I leaned on to drive profits. But, during extended periods of low volatility or sideways markets, I would be more likely to use a form of the house approach to keep the pennies rolling in. Yumiko tried to use the player approach to take advantage of a market view, a special situation that her understanding of markets took her towards. However, she was not skilled in running long-term risk within the structure of a player approach, and her trading reflexes were not geared towards this type of trading.

The danger is that we rarely see the boundaries, and do not always have clarity around them. I would sometimes forget myself and start trading the house approach as a way of making money for longer periods, usually at my own expense.

That said there are people who are doing both approaches, they are usually very experienced traders. And there may be times where it is possible and viable to do both. Amongst some of the situations where I have seen successful hybrids, the traders have been very clear that one trade or strategy fits in with a certain approach. The traders set different rules, use different sizing approaches, apply different risk management philosophies. They also run the trades as separate trading portfolios.

I am however deliberately avoiding discussing the hybrid approach at length, as it could take me, and this book, down all sorts of rabbit holes. As a reminder, less is more, is part of the philosophy of this book.

THE BARGAIN WITH THE SELF

A bargain with your self helps you to keep your self on your side by laying out the terms that it will have to agree to when you apply your approach. The aim of this is to enable you to bring the best version of your self with you at all times.

As a reminder, most traders' playbooks exist inside their heads, thus the bargain is mostly implicit. On the other hand, it can be useful to write your playbook out – giving the bargain physical form and making it 'explicit'.

If your self cannot agree to the bargain, problems are likely to become baked-in. At a later stage you may then find yourself thinking "I didn't sign up for this." This is what Yumiko said she was thinking when we discussed how she felt during her trade. It is part of a trader's reflective work, and 'soul-searching' to flesh out these matters. In the latter part of the book, we explore journalling as a tool to help with these matters.

WHICH APPROACH SHOULD YOU USE?

I do not consider either approach to be superior to the other, but there will be times when one of them is more appropriate. The house approach is quicker and simpler to learn, and most new traders adopt a basic variation of it for that reason at the beginning of their trading career.

Most traders in proprietary firms use variations of the house approach. The basic house approach can produce quick profits if the conditions are right.

Traders in market-making positions within banks, commodity, and energy trading would be expected to utilise the house approach to optimise their performance as liquidity providers. By doing so, they can effectively leverage their firm's (house's) edge and achieve their mandate to provide liquidity or move physical product while making a profit. This will be explored in more detail in the next chapter.

The player approach, and more sophisticated versions of the house approach, will be beyond the capability of most new and novice traders. Both require a high degree of experience and the development of specialist and tacit knowledge. This is another reason why learning a house-approach style is a good starting point. It gives the trader the chance to develop the knowledge and gain the experience needed to progress later.

Market conditions and other market factors may also be a consideration.

Many house-approach styles have a shelf-life. Some house-approach systems can work well for a few years, then suddenly stop working as conditions change. Pit traders were house-approach traders, but the terrain of their markets changed as electronic trading replaced open-outcry trading, and most did not have the right reflexes or skills for the new terrain.

Player approaches usually have greater longevity and adaptability across markets and market conditions. House approaches are usually very specific – the trader becomes an expert in one market. Exceptions here are more advanced specialist house approaches, which include portfolio management approaches, management of complex derivative portfolios, long-short methods and relative value approaches, and some directional trend-following and discretionary styles.

The following describes some of the key aspects of the two approaches.

PLAYER APPROACH

SOME KEY CHARACTERISTICS

- Asymmetric styles with relatively larger wins among many small or breakeven trades.

- Capital is used selectively and applied aggressively to favourable setups.

- Trades occur sporadically and unpredictably.

- Traders typically search for low-risk/high-reward setups.

- There can be long periods of inactivity, and profit can bleed during these periods.

- Risk management is usually very specific to a single trade. Traders tend to use stop strategies or committed amounts of capital.

- Player-approach traders typically look at how much they are willing to lose (put at risk) on a trade, in order to establish risk size.

- The player approach is considered a long-volatility approach, much like being long of options – the downside is limited.

TYPICAL STYLES

Short-term: intraday swing-trading; event-driven approaches; sniping strategies.

Medium-term: swing/macro-trading strategies; momentum trading; trend-following; contrarian approaches; strategic position-taking approaches; directional spread trading.

Long-term: macro with a directional bias; value investing; absolute return approaches.

HOUSE APPROACH

SOME KEY CHARACTERISTICS

- Typically, many relatively small wins among a few occasional larger losses.

- Can be considered as analogous to 'picking up pennies in front of a steamroller'.

- Capital allocated to high-intensity systematic, semi-systematic, or mean reversion portfolio approaches.

- Intensive and highly active trading style with constant or near-constant exposure.

- Typically, the house's edge favours this approach, though usually in a market-making or physical product franchise business.

- Traders seek to avoid, or hedge against, tail-events – the 'sting in the fat-tail'.

- Risk management is often generic and applied across a portfolio. Stops may be used on individual trades but can be counterproductive to this approach.

- The house approach is considered a short-volatility approach, much like going short of an option – the downside is unlimited.

- Sizing is normally based on the trader's specific size preference, or that allowed by their mandate or their own rules.

TYPICAL STYLES

Short-term: scalping; high-frequency trading; market-making; highly liquid market flow-trading. Day to day liquidity management of physical product portfolios, assets and liabilities.

Medium-term: relative value basis trading; arbitrage; market-making less liquid markets; strategic position-taking approaches within a franchise or portfolio. Management of physical product portfolios, assets and liabilities.

Long-term: relative value approaches; long/short strategies; most factor investing approaches; portfolio approaches.

In the next chapter, the final one of this foundational section, I introduce the idea of positive expectancy or edge, and some of the sources of edge for traders who are working in sell-side roles and buy-side roles.

CHAPTER 7

Positive Expectancy – Edge

Few people ever make money on tips. Beware of inside information. If there was easy money lying around, no one would be forcing it into your pocket.

Jesse Livermore, legendary trader

IN JANUARY 2015 the Swiss National Bank (SNB) stunned markets when they decided to abandon the currency peg which held the Swiss franc firmly within a tight band against the euro – the currency used by the European Union.

A currency peg ties a country's currency to a specific exchange rate with another currency to help stabilise its value, which promotes growth and reduces investment risk. The central bank maintains the rate by buying or selling its currency in the foreign exchange market.

The SNB had maintained an exchange rate at 1.20 Swiss francs to the euro for over three years. In a chaotic few minutes after the announcement, the Swiss franc soared by around 30% in value against the euro.

The move caused drama in bank and hedge fund trading rooms across the world. At the time I was coaching the traders at a bank in London.

The bank was not usually highly active in trading the Swiss franc; however, prior to this event they had one large speculative trade on and some Swiss franc orders from clients which needed monitoring.

The large speculative trade was from a proprietary trader at the bank, who had been running a long euro versus Swiss franc (EURCHF) FX position, to the tune of EUR 100 million. The income from this trade was minor; however, placed in large size, and supposedly locked into a pegged currency relationship, which was trading close the base of the pegged currency band, it seemed like a free call-option.

In the days prior to the SNB moves, the bank's head of trading – a very experienced trader – had picked up on some nuance in commentary on the EURCHF that caused him some concern.

At the time there was a lot of selling pressure on the EURCHF currency pair. However, the SNB had re-affirmed their commitment to maintaining the EURCHF currency peg.

The bank's head of trading, through experience, had learned to be sceptical of central bank commitments. Asking one of his traders to exit a position went against his principles, but on this occasion something just did not feel right. He asked the proprietary trader with the EURCHF to exit the trade.

After some protest, the trader closed his position, using the bank's own FX traders. The head of the FX traders asked him why he was exiting now. He mentioned the concerns the head of trading had expressed. The head of the FX traders, mindful of the potential for something unexpected to happen, cautioned his own traders to be alert to any potential exposure that may cause them to be short of the Swiss franc.

A couple of days later, the SNB withdrew from the Swiss franc peg.

Immediately, the price of the EURCHF dropped 1%. Then, for a few brief seconds, the market froze, liquidity had evaporated, there were no prices in the market. A few, much lower, bids remained, possibly from automated market-makers – trading firms that agree to always have a bid or offer in the market. But for a trader to hit a bid 100 or 200 ticks below the last price, in a market that usually had a one-tick spread, seemed unfathomable.

However, alerted by the concerns of the head of trading, the traders at the bank did not freeze. They sold.

The traders hit whatever bids were there. The price then plummeted, but not by 100 or 200 ticks: the market dropped 1600 ticks to 1.0200, though liquidity was so bad that some systems had the next trade as low as 0.8600. (Note; these prices do not appear on most charts of the price action that day, due to the extremely thin volumes traded.)

There was carnage in the market. Some banks and hedge funds were reported to have suffered losses in the hundreds of millions of dollars. But for the bank where I was coaching, it was estimated that the proactive trading on the FX desk made them around EUR 5m trading profit on the day. In addition, where customers at other banks were being 'hung out to dry' on their orders, this bank was able to fulfil all its customer orders at the levels they had requested.

Far more significantly, the actions of the head of trading – whose instincts had caused him to ask the trader to exit the large speculative EURCHF position – had saved the bank at least EUR 30m.

This story emphasises the sell-side trader's edge. The bank did not have any inside or advance information, but it had a group of experienced traders and a head of trading who listened to his intuition – his 'tacit knowledge' honed over three decades in the markets.

EDGE

A positive expectancy – or edge – occurs when the approach used by a trader generates an outcome in which the aggregate value of all the expected wins exceeds the aggregate value of the expected losses.

In the blackjack trading analogy, the house has a positive expectancy in the aggregate of their transactions. That is the house's edge. They just need to follow a systematic method or system in order to monetise it. Players, by contrast, have the edge against them; they have a negative expectancy. Despite this, skilled gamers use strategies such as card counting to create a more positive expectancy for themselves.

I will use the FX market to explore how the blackjack trading analogy applies to trading. From here onwards in this chapter, and to avoid confusion, I will use the term 'buy-side traders' in place of the term 'players' and the term 'sell-side traders' in place of 'the house'. Use of the term 'player approach' and 'house approach' will remain.

THE SELL-SIDE EDGE

In the FX market, the market-makers – traders who show bids and offers to the market so that people can gain access to the markets, are predominantly working for the banks. A bank's market-makers exist in their trading room. These market-making traders are akin to the dealers at the blackjack table: they are playing on behalf of the house (the bank).

The banks' approach, like the casinos', is to try to monetise their edge where it exists. Occasionally, the banks will take a hit, though generally they try to keep their relative exposure on the low side. They manage their risk carefully, angling it in ways which allow them to capitalise on the edges they have.

Bank traders have several edges. As with the casino, individually these edges are small – even negligible – but with sufficient volume, turnover and use of skilled approaches, they combine and compound them to produce a significant return.

EDGE FROM THE SPREAD

The spread on currency transactions (the difference between what a trader will pay for a currency and what they will sell it for in the FX market), though very tight, provides a source of income for banks. Though the tight spreads produce negligible profits individually, the banks actively aggregate tens of thousands of transactions daily using electronic aggregating systems, to provide an accumulated effect. Very large trades still go through the traders, who fulfil the transactions in the market, while attempting to capture a small spread on the currency transaction for their own P&L.

The increased commoditisation of the currency markets has made this edge increasingly negligible in the major currencies, but wider spreads still exist on less liquid currencies. In fact, so thin is the edge that trading with some of the larger players in the market, such as central banks and hedge funds, may be more expensive than the spread benefit warrants. In these circumstances a bank will often complete the trade regardless, with the view that the value is found in building and sustaining relationships with such players.

EDGE FROM FLOW INFORMATION

More important to the traders is information from the flow of transactions. Bank traders are constantly engaged in making prices to the market. This activity provides useful clues as to where liquidity exists. Liquidity is the lifeblood of any market. Skilful house-approach traders learn how to milk the liquidity in their market.

Other terms for this include 'reading the tape', 'reading the order-flow', 'reading order books' and 'ladder trading'.

Many highly skilled retail traders become masters at reading the flow. They adopt scalping strategies, which they transact with fast, intuitive-style trading. To do this, they need to be in the market constantly to assess and feel the flow. This is one of the challenges of house-approach trading: it is hard to switch off and requires constant attention.

EDGE FROM MARKET CENTRICITY

Traders at banks sit in the very epicentre of the markets. They are positioned among a constant flow of information, market orders, data, research, news and opinions coming from analysts, newswires and financial news programmes. They sit close to other traders in related roles, products and markets, and near to salespeople engaging with clients. They also receive regular insights and opinions from brokers, customers, counterparts and colleagues in overseas offices.

This creates a febrile atmosphere, which itself becomes a fantastic source of sensory information for the switched on, engaged and present trader. This is the benefit of being in a high-turnover, high-volume business.

On one occasion one of my futures brokers, Justin Waller, took me to what was then the LIFFE floor (London's open outcry futures exchange – now ICE Futures Europe) and introduced me to some of the pit traders. It was the morning the US non-farm payroll data – the world's most significant monthly economic data – was released. In the days leading up to each release of the data, all the talk in bank trading rooms is about how the market will react to the various possible outcomes.

On my visit to the LIFFE floor, I asked the pit traders if they had any market expectations for the data release. They both looked at me like I was mad. They knew the data was coming out, but they did not care what the data was; they would just watch the flows when they happened. They were at the very epicentre of the markets. This *was* their edge. They would read the terrain of the markets as they traversed it – having a map (a guiding opinion) could only be counterproductive.

KNOWLEDGE EXPOSURE EDGE
– TACIT KNOWLEDGE

Tacit knowledge is implicit, rather than explicit. It is knowledge that is difficult to express or state, and thus extremely difficult to describe in tangible terms. It is the mysterious knowledge, often called intuition or gut-feel, that results from experience, received wisdom and observation – combined with accumulated explicit knowledge and learning.

Market-makers must be constantly vigilant against attacks from large speculative traders, such as hedge funds and other market-makers. They are working in near-random environments, characterised by radical uncertainty, where unexpected and unpredictable events occur without warning. (The 'without warning' part of that sentence may seem superfluous, but my intuitive sense is that it felt necessary to mention.)

A market-maker needs to develop a way of being 'proactively defensive'. This proactive defensiveness eventually imbues the successful market-maker with intuitive abilities that get them ahead of fast and volatile markets.

This is the most significant individual edge of all, and forms a formidable part of the house's edge within a bank or sell-side firm.

THE BUY-SIDE EDGE

The buy-side trader's edge is market intelligence, explicit knowledge and tacit knowledge combined, or the successful application of a sophisticated house-approach system. Sometimes it is a combination of all of these things.

Explicit knowledge alone is not an edge. In markets, every piece of this form of knowledge you have is available to everyone else. The exceptions occur in low-liquidity markets, but that knowledge edge eventually disappears, or may be on the wrong side of what is legally acceptable. Without tacit knowledge, a trader does not have a sustainable process.

Systematic approaches are similar. They reduce the edge against a buy-side trader, but they alone do not eliminate it. The trader's tacit knowledge then adds to the system, whether at the point of execution with superior discretionary decisions adding to systematic signals received, or in the design, build and management of the system, adding a unique aspect which is difficult to identify from the scanning of data, or explicit knowledge of the product or market.

The buy-side trader's edge comes from tacit knowledge gained through lived experience as a trader (often in a sell-side role originally), allied to a system or method and the base of explicit knowledge a good trader has developed.

Part One has given you an overview of the Performance Process Cycle and other essential components required to master the mental game of trading. The subsequent parts of this book, Parts Two through Five, will delve deeper into the cycle, with each section focusing on a particular quadrant.

PART TWO

THE PERFORMANCE PROCESS CYCLE – QUADRANT 1

CHAPTER 8

The 'Being' Phase

Empty your mind, be formless. Shapeless, like water. If you put water into a cup, it becomes the cup. You put water into a bottle and it becomes the bottle. You put it in a teapot it becomes the teapot. Now, water can flow or it can crash. Be water, my friend.

Bruce Lee, martial artists and actor

A S WE PROGRESS through the next four parts of the book, each one focuses on a specific quadrant of the Performance Process Cycle. The themes explored in each part are relevant to that quadrant, providing a deeper understanding of each phase and some of the themes which arise for traders during those phases.

To aid in this process, the first chapter of each part provides an in-depth examination of the quadrant in question. To illustrate the concepts covered, I have chosen to use one specific trade as an example throughout this book. This example illuminates some of the concepts discussed in each section, helping to cement your understanding of the ideas and themes presented.

This trade is the one that I consider to be my best ever in terms of how well I planned, structured, executed and managed it, as well as how I handled myself throughout the process. The trade was one I executed in May 2007. Specifically, it was a short position I initiated in the German Government Bond Futures contract, commonly known as the Bund. While this trade was far from being the biggest or most profitable of my career, it was the one that personally brought me the most satisfaction.

THE BEING PHASE

This phase of the cycle gives life and power to the trading process. Here, the trader prepares for the coming trade or trading decision.

The Being Phase is not an active part of the trading process; its purpose is to prime the trader to be in an optimal state of being which enables them to transact and effect their process most productively. While this quadrant does not involve any of the transactional parts of the trade, such as idea generation, planning, execution or risk management, it is vital in the formulation of good process, and gives power to the trader and their process – hence we term it a Power Zone.

The quote from Bruce Lee at the start of this chapter captures the essence of the Being Phase. I once had the pleasure of visiting a Bruce Lee exhibition on a visit to Hong Kong. These words formed a central theme of the exhibition and have stayed with me ever since. They also reside at the core of the Being Phase. In short, "be water, my friend" – adaptable and open minded.

Figure 20: Power Zone 1

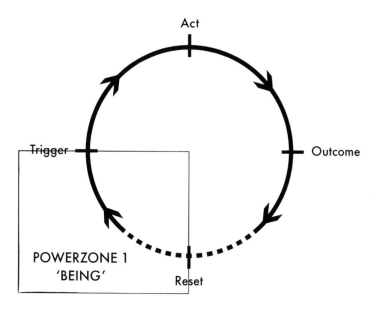

STARTING WITH PURPOSE – THE WHY AND THE WAY

At the start of any trading process, it is essential for traders to check in with themselves and remind themselves of their purpose. Their purpose is their 'why', their reason and rationale for trading. This also involves updating themselves on how they plan to achieve their purpose and the steps they will take to make it happen. This is referred to as their 'way'.

The why and the way inform the trader's strategy, tactics, rules and guidelines that they will use to fulfil their purpose. Those elements form their playbook.

While it would not be reasonable to expect you to do this at every step of the process, bringing the purpose to mind regularly, particularly at the start of the day, focuses your energy on your task.

Having a clear and singular sense of purpose powers the trader's process, providing a compelling rationale to keep the trader on track. Contrast that with a trader who enters a cycle without clarity of purpose – they will be much more vulnerable to deviating from the cycle and veering off-process. This could be the start of a spiralling behaviour that may ultimately result in a complete breakdown of their trading strategy as they enter a 'death spiral'. As you read through the book, I will provide you with multiple real-world examples of this concept, further solidifying your understanding of these ideas.

As a proprietary trader, my why – and therefore my purpose – was to take risks in the Macro Markets (Bond, Interest Rate and Currency/FX markets), to generate a profit or return in a way which protected or limited my downside so that losses were contained and did not accumulate to a point where I would have to stop trading.

My playbook focused on finding asymmetric risk-reward opportunities in the markets I traded. I accepted a low win rate, and occasional periods of underperformance and P&L bleed as the compromise, and thus as part of 'my bargain', in this activity.

My way involved using a variety of analytical practices to identify setups. These included fundamental and technical analysis as well as my own intuitive reading of the market, whereby I would try to identify the market sentiment and its current drivers. I placed my trades prudently, applying the basic tenets of risk management while respecting the bank's risk rules and the mandate it had given to me.

OPTIMAL TRADER STATE AND FLOW STATE

When a trader is present to, and focused on, their trading task or activity, they can be described as being in an 'optimal trader state'. The idea of being present throughout the entire trading is so central to outstanding performance that it forms what I consider to be one of the three Ps of high performance. I expand on this in the next chapter.

Being 'present' is a far higher level of being than merely being engaged. Being present requires focus in the present moment, with mindful awareness of your thoughts, actions, and surroundings. This includes being fully immersed in the moment, giving your complete attention to your actions, as well as the action of others around you and who you are engaged with, and being aware of the broader context and situations at play.

Since markets are the collective and aggregated actions of others playing the same game as you, being present to the behaviours of markets, both from an external and internal perspective, is part of being present as a trader.

Being in an Optimal Trader State is the condition I aim for whenever I commence the trading process. A trader in an Optimal Trader State has a clear and coherent sense of purpose and is free of biases, distractions, strong beliefs and attachments. They are not hindered by the baggage of prior trades or previous narratives. Crucially their ego is a driver of success, motivating them to succeed and act appropriately to win, rather than interfering in their process and diminishing their ability to be present, and holding them back from practising curiosity.

Being in an optimal trader state gives a trader a greater chance of executing their process effectively as they progress around the cycle and navigating their way through the uncertainty of markets.

A trader in this state is able to exercise their full mental capital. They are energetically available for the challenges they face and can act with fluid responsiveness to events and disturbances as they unfold.

Maintaining an optimal trader state can however be physically draining, which is why rationing time, taking breaks and being in peak physical and mental condition is vital.

Once in an optimal trader state, a trader has a greater chance of achieving the ultimate state it is possible for them to reach: a 'flow state'.

In a flow state trading feels effortless and timeless. The trader is completely at one with their self as they face the outer game. Their ego is silenced – out of the picture. In a flow state mental capital remains high – it does not erode or deplete.

A trader cannot will themselves into a flow state, and achieving it is rare, but starting from an optimal trader state makes it more likely to occur. It also makes them more resilient, more able to remain on-process, and less likely to be hijacked or sabotaged by their ego. They are more able to effectively monetise favourable situations and recover more quickly when they slip, lapse or suffer setbacks. They are also more able to learn, grow, integrate experiences, adapt and evolve.

Achieving an optimal trader state does not just happen. It requires the trader to apply deliberate effort and make a commitment to excellence, as well as accepting their own fallibility.

SUB-OPTIMAL TRADER STATE AND TILT STATE

While the aim for a trader is to begin a trade or a trading process from an optimal trader state, traders spend much of their time in a sub-optimal trader state. Quite simply, if you want to win this extremely difficult and challenging game of trading, it is vital to be in an optimal trader state as often as possible. This makes it important for a trader to be able to identify when they are slipping towards a sub-optimal trader state – or are already in one.

When a trader is in a sub-optimal trader state, they may lack the necessary focus on their purpose and how to achieve it, their ability to be present is far lower, and they are more susceptible to ego-driven behaviours. This can lead to deviation from the Performance Process

Cycle and hinder the trader's ability to sustain high-level performance. While they may still be generating profits, their behaviours may not be aligned with optimal performance, increasing the likelihood of future underperformance.

The deeper a trader slips into a sub-optimal trader state, the more at risk they are of falling further, into a 'tilt state' (taken from the poker terminology). When in a tilt state, poor performance is pretty much guaranteed. In a tilt state, trying to shake-off the pattern of continual poor performance becomes difficult.

All traders are liable to fall into a sub-optimal trader state and everyone at some point is fallible to entering into a tilt state. A lack of deliberate effort or commitment to growth and lazy thinking increases the odds of this happening.

IMMERSION AND SENSING

A further aspect of the Being phase, and more directly related to the physical and transactional aspect of a trade are 'immersion' and 'sensing'.

Immersion is the outer-game aspect of the Being Phase. The trader commits to full immersion in the market. They observe the market, watch the price action, follow the news, assess the market sentiment, gather information, assess data, read research, share and receive views and opinions with others.

The effectiveness of this immersion will be helped by the quality of the questions the trader asks of the market, the situation and the environment. They should be exercising a deep level of curiosity to understand what is happening, not merely observing. They should be asking about what is moving and driving markets, what are the underlying factors which are affecting the market, and what are other market particpants thinking as the news and price action unfolds.

The trader's ability to ask questions of the market will be impacted by the state of their relationship with their self.

At the same time as the trader engages with their outer game in this way, they are also engaging their inner game by gauging, feeling and intuiting what is happening – this is the sensing element of the Being Phase.

While sensing, it is important to retain a stance of, and practise, 'detached curiosity'. This is something we explore a little further on in this part of the book. Detached curiosity is a state of mind in which you can ask questions without being attached to the implications they may have for your ego. It is a non-ego state that allows for objective inquiry and a willingness to explore without personal biases or attachment.

Removing the ego's influence at this time is important because the Being Phase is the well from which the trader's ideas and actions emerge and where their energy, in the form of mental capital, is stored. When the ego interferes in the being phase, the trader can become desensitised to the information coming from the market, reducing their level of insight. This also drains energy, depleting the trader's mental capital. The well of a desensitised trader contains less insight and lower levels of mental capital.

THE BEING PHASE AND FAILURE TO LET GO

As we explored in Chapter 2, if a trader has failed to complete the Letting Go Phase of a previous cycle, they will have been unable to ground and reset, and will not be able to re-enter the Being Phase. Instead they will jump directly back to the Performance Phase (acting without thinking).

When this occurs it corrupts their Performance Process Cycle and sends them into a non-productive cycle. This is what happened to

Yumiko in the previous chapter. The non-productive cycle put Yumiko into a deep sub-optimal trader state, from which she entered a spiralling behaviour and subsequently the dreaded death spiral where she found herself in a full-tilt mindset. First she surrendered potential gains, then she traded poorly and erratically while spurning more opportunities.

In the next chapter, we will look at another example in which this happened to a trader. But first, let us return to my May 2007 Bund trade in relation to the Being Phase.

THE BEING PHASE AND THE MAY 2007 BUND TRADE

The first few months of 2007 had not been good to me, yet despite my profit and loss (P&L) statement being negative for the year, I was in a calm place. Some of my trade ideas that year had failed, and I had not yet hit upon a winning trade. While this was concerning, this is how my approach plays out, and is part of the psychological bargain I made with myself: I presume that patience will eventually be rewarded, and a winning trade will come along.

My analysis had identified a potential for a favourable risk-reward setup on the Bund. This was based on a chart pattern I had been watching for several months and my own intuitive feeling about the market.

Twice since the start of March I had attempted to enter a long-yield play on the German Government Bond (which required shorting Bund futures), but I had to book losses on both trades when the market failed to follow through.

I had not abandoned that trade idea, but I was not overly committed to it either. I try not to remain attached to my prevailing view, preferring to be considered neither bullish nor bearish; this way I am able to exercise detached curiosity and avoid being co-opted into any market 'tribe'. This may change once a trade is in play, but in the Being Phase it is vital for me to be open to all options. Or, as Bruce Lee said, "be water, my friend."

Crucially, I knew my why and my way. Despite being in the red, I remained in an optimal trader state and was fully immersed in the market – watching the news, the flow, the price action. I was sensing the market and primed for any opportunities.

I will pick up this story of the May 2007 trade in the introduction to Part Three, where the Performance Process Cycle enters the Production Phase. In the remaining chapters of Part 2, the book explores some of the themes and concepts raised in this chapter in greater detail, commencing with a more detailed look at the 3Ps of High Performance.

CHAPTER 9

Trading, the Ego and the 3Ps of High Performance

Don't have an ego. Always question yourself and your ability. Don't ever feel that you are very good. The second you do, you are dead.

Paul Tudor-Jones, legendary trader and hedge fund manager

I T WAS THE end of January 2022. Although the year had just started, Tony felt like it was already over. He sat in his chair, head buried in his hands, traumatised and barely able to bring himself to move. He could not face the act of getting up, turning out the lights in his office and walking out the door. That would make the events of the past few weeks real.

So, Tony remained sitting there long into the evening, trying to fathom out how he had managed to get it so wrong. How, in the space of a few short weeks, had he turned what seemed to be a triumph into such a disaster?

Tony had been up several million dollars on a bitcoin trade heading into the final months of 2021. It was all going so well. Unlike many in the cryptocurrency markets of 2020 and 2021, Tony was not new to trading, which made the current outcome all the worse for him. "I should have known better," he said.

Tony was a retail trader who had started trading in 2005. After a few challenging, unproductive years, he finally started to make some money in the volatile markets of 2008. He then built his trading career on the back of that.

Tony became attracted to crypto in the late 2010s, but 2020 was the year in which he started to make significant trading profits.

2021 had been a rocky ride; the second quarter had seen a major correction in the dollar price of bitcoin from the $60,000 level to close to $30,000, but Tony managed to negotiate this correction well and actually made some money on the move lower.

As the market appeared to base near $30,000, he started to sense that the bull move may re-assert itself. He felt the possibility of bitcoin recovering back to (or beyond) its highs was strong, so he positioned himself for that move.

In the second half of 2021, the move he had been hoping for unfolded. Tony was long of bitcoin, and as the move gathered steam he increased his position. He was making a lot of money. Buoyed by his success, and confident that this was going to pan out as he predicted, he increased his risk further. This increase in his risk size was to be his undoing.

A cornerstone of Tony's success had been strict sizing and position criteria; he had always adhered to this. This enabled him to make decent money on his views but kept him safe when unexpected events occurred or when he was just plain wrong.

During the strong run-up in bitcoin in 2021, Tony started to loosen his rules around money management. As the profits started to roll in, this approach seemed vindicated. His confidence surged, and his prudential risk management was almost totally abandoned. Tony normally limited his risk to 5% of his capital, but on this trade he now had 50% of his capital at risk. Tony has no longer a predefined stop level where he could value any potential losses. As such, he had not realised quite how exposed he was.

By early November 2021, bitcoin was above $60,000. Tony was sitting on a $5m-plus profit on that trade alone, more than ten times his best-ever year.

Tony engaged in conversations with other crypto traders. The buzz was all about $100,000 bitcoin. The talk was frenetic; Tony summarised it as: "It was not even a question of if, but when."

Tony's head had been turned. He had dollar signs in his eyes. His thoughts turned to what car he would buy, what house he could own. If he was up over $5m here, that could be $15m or even $20m in a few months' time.

Discipline, structure and process went out the window. What could possibly go wrong?

The market moved higher, getting close to $70,000, then some profit-taking in mid-November brought it back to below $60,000.

'HODL', the slang abbreviation for 'hold on for dear life' used by the crypto-trading crowd (the 'hodlers') to advise a buy-and-hold indefinitely strategy, was being bandied about by everyone. Tony used to loathe this phrase, but by this point he had become a dedicated follower. "That should have been the clue," he later said to me.

The market dropped a little further. "Guys, there is free money here," one chatgroup host shouted out. Tony considered it, but he knew he was maxed out on leverage. November ended, and Tony remained confident.

Then, in the space of less than 24 hours at the start of December, bitcoin collapsed from $57,000 to an intraday low of $42,000, before rebounding sharply to near $50,000.

Tony's profit evaporated. He had increased his size on the way up, and his average long was near 47,000.

Tony was shellshocked. The bounce of the lows meant he was still slightly in profit, but he did not know what to do now. He froze as he watched his hopes, desires, dreams, and the profits which had fuelled them evaporate. In the end he convinced himself that he should stay long. "The market's done this before. It'll base, just stay in there," he said to himself. Everyone he spoke to was saying the same.

The market spent the rest of December in a sideways range. This convinced him, or at least he convinced himself, it would rally in the new year. Then in January 2022 bitcoin sunk below 40,000. Tony had finally had enough. He could not stomach the idea of a margin call, so he sold out. He had lost more than $1m on the trade, depleting a large part of his capital in the process.

Tony has very generously allowed me to tell this story, though at his request I have not used his real name.

Before I analyse Tony's situation, I would like to explore a concept, already referred to in the last chapter, which will be central to our journey around the Performance Process Cycle. It is what I call the '3Ps of High Performance'. The 3Ps are 'presence', 'purpose' and 'process'.

THE 3PS OF HIGH PERFORMANCE

In order to achieve high performance you must learn to keep your ego tame so that it does not impair your results. A tame ego allows you to work with its 'bright side' – the part that drives you forward – while the 'dark side' – which wants to interfere with the task at hand – remains at bay. To do this you must work to maintain the 3Ps of high performance, purpose, process and presence. Each one of these needs to be attended to, both in their own right and in support of each other.

Figure 21: The 3Ps of High Performance

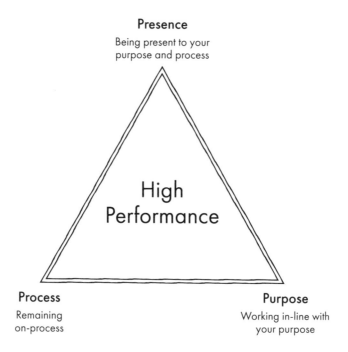

The first of these is purpose. Your purpose is the reason you are doing this. When you are working with purpose, it is easier to stay on-process and remain present.

The second 'P' is process. Your process must be carried out in a way which enables you to fulfil your purpose and which supports your ability to remain present.

The third is presence. In this context, being present means bringing the best version of your self to the process and applying it to achieve your purpose.

Successful application of the 3Ps enables you to mobilise the positive attributes of your ego without being undermined by its negative aspects. Left unchecked, these negative aspects release powerful emotions that disrupt your ability to remain present, cause you to veer off-process and hijack your purpose.

I view the 3Ps of High Performance as a triangle, with each component supporting the others. Together they keep the ego tame, at bay outside the boundaries of performance.

Figure 22: The 3Ps and the ego

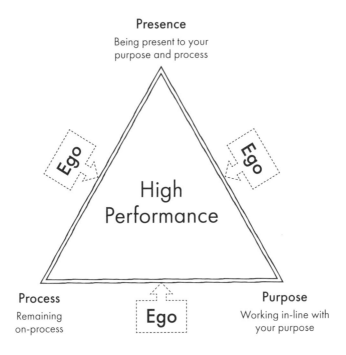

TONY'S TRADE

Tony's trade did not go wrong when bitcoin turned down. The cracks were already there; it just needed a catalyst to prise the cracks wide open.

In reality the trade went wrong when his ego became involved in his process, and he abandoned his trusted money-management practices. Tony lost the mental game at that moment. He did have a chance to recover it, but this is even harder to do when you are making money, because everything seems right.

This is an example of a point made in the previous chapter on the Being Phase, that the erosion in performance does not always occur simultaneously to sub-optimal behaviours being practised. While a trader may still be generating profits, their behaviours may not be aligned with optimal performance, increasing the likelihood of future underperformance.

In Tony's case, as he abandoned his process and the principles which are part of his process, his trading went from a focus on high performance to a focus on 'ego-led performance'. He started playing to the crowd.

'Playing to the crowd' means to act, behave or perform in such a way as to receive as much approval from an audience or group of spectators as one can get – especially from the lowest common denominator therein. Keep in mind that your ego tends to assume that there are external peers who are aware of your thoughts and actions, even if this may not necessarily be the case.

But as it happened, there was a crowd Tony had been playing to. His fellow hodlers loved Tony, and he loved the companionship and support they showed him. Or rather, his ego did.

Tony's is another story of a trader who moved onto an unproductive cycle then descended into a sub-optimal trader state – even though performance was still good.

This is why trading is so hard: it is a mental game, a performance activity, not an academic or transactional one.

Many traders, and particularly those in the early years of their career, make the mistake of assuming that trading success comes from gaining knowledge and technical expertise. However, this way of thinking is flawed because when they encounter challenges, they believe that acquiring more knowledge and technical skills will solve the problem, or that they should have seen something 'unpredictable' coming. In reality, persistent failures in trading are rarely due to a lack of knowledge or technical skills.

No matter how extensive the knowledge, or how hard the trader is working to win, it is usually their temperament that lets them down.

Victor Sperandeo said in Jack D. Schwager's *New Market Wizards* (HarperBusiness, 1992), "The key to trading success is emotional discipline. If intelligence were the key, there would be a lot more people making money trading."

The factors which contribute to success have less to do with academic acumen and far more to do with the factors that lead to success in sport, music, acting and art. You cannot learn to swim, cycle or walk a tightrope from a book, and the same is true of trading.

Trading falls into a unique performance category.

Perhaps the closest of the other performance categories is that of card games like poker and bridge, those with an almost infinite number of possibilities and many of the same mental skills required to succeed. Not surprisingly, many poker and bridge players thrive as traders.

NO SIMPLE SOLUTIONS

In the chapter on behavioural slippage, I noted how the behaviours that traders identify as failures are usually not the cause of their inability to succeed. The issues which cause these symptoms are often complex and varied, and many have their roots in the tangled relationship between us, our self and our ego.

It is also important to recognise that relying solely on a valid system or method with a positive expectancy does not guarantee success. You have a strong outer game and a positive outlook, but may still struggle to achieve success if you cannot remain committed to the process so that you can monetise that positive expectancy.

Staying on-process is hard, particularly when the ego is triggered and wants to control the host.

Even when the ego is contained, it is always looking for a chance to break free and take control of the host's actions. This is what happened to Tony. His problems stemmed from the erosion of his process, his presence and his purpose.

Tony had built a process which powered his success for many years and served him well. It kept his ego constrained. But the ego eventually found a way in and took control of Tony's trading.

By stealth, it managed to get its hands on the reins. Then away it went, causing havoc like a five-ton wrecking ball. This is what self-sabotage looks like. The ego sabotages the efforts of the self.

Managing your ego is no easy task. The ego wants instant results and big wins, not the patient application of process. Nor does it want the many hours, days, weeks, even years spent learning, building and refining a process capable of winning.

Tony's story is an example of how your ego can sabotage you, your performance, possibly even your career. I am glad to say that Tony has started to make progress again in his trading. But his confidence took a big hit, and recovery is a slow process.

CHAPTER 10

What the Market Wants for You

My favourite chip trick is to make everyone's chip stack disappear!

Amarillo Slim, legendary poker champion

WARREN WAS A young trader at a prop trading firm. He was doing relatively well but felt he had significant untapped potential.

He shared with me a list of issues he was encountering. These were the typical cocktail of behaviours which I prefer to label as symptoms rather than causes: taking profit too quickly; running losses too far; panicking; hesitating; getting sucked in by FOMO; lacking discipline; impatience, and so on. The unforced errors of trading.

I was keen to get past these unforced errors and explore below the surface, to gauge what might be happening at a deeper level.

Warren had a strong process, which he had learned on the training programme at the prop firm, reinforced by some excellent mentoring from a fellow trader who had taken him under his wing. He used a fast and aggressive day-trading approach, but something seemed to be triggering his ego and sabotaging his ability to fully play his edge out.

I asked Warren probing questions but often found a wall of resistance. He would deflect my questions and act evasively. This made it difficult to get below the surface. Warren was not giving a lot away, and I found myself getting frustrated. Then, in one session, he casually said, "I think I might have a better week next week."

"Why do you think that?" I asked.

"Because Roy is away," he replied with some glee.

My curiosity was piqued. I asked who Roy was and why Warren expected his absence to help.

It turned out that Roy was a colleague who constantly irritated Warren and seemed to take pleasure in winding him up.

When I suggested that this may be why Warren was not achieving what he felt was his potential, he was dismissive of this.

I pointed out that he had said he felt his chances would be better in the next week, when Roy was not going to be around, and that this seemed to indicate there would be less behavioural slippage for him because Roy would be away.

On the face of it, it seemed like Roy was the issue.

Sometimes, when we get annoyed by someone, it might be because that person is toxic. Alternatively, it could be that we are responding to them with toxicity, and the problem is one that we have generated.

I asked him if he had similar issues with other people, either now or in the past. To my surprise, he reeled off a string of examples from both trading and other parts of his life.

So perhaps Roy was not the problem; he was just the catalyst for a deeper issue manifesting.

It seemed that Warren allowed other people inside his head far too easily. He allowed their egos to trigger his ego. This often caused his performance to become ego-led rather than high-performance focused.

This will be less of a problem for traders who have a strong relationship with their self or are well aligned with their core self. But it turned out that Warren's relationship with his self was somewhat challenging.

Paradoxically, this was what made it difficult for me to help Warren. His ego was getting in the way of my coaching. It wanted me to work on his trading – his outer game – at the surface level rather than digging deeper. It was trying to keep me out.

As the conversation continued, Warren became a little more comfortable opening up, but he still struggled to do so fully. Nonetheless, as we delved further below the surface, he revealed that he never fully trusted himself and often expected bad outcomes to happen to him. When people feel this way, they are prone to act with hesitation and too much caution – which in Warren's case ran counter to his trading approach.

Bringing these issues into the open proved helpful for Warren. We explored ways he could deal with the immediate problem. We came up with a 'tripwire', which is a tool or mechanism deployed when matters take a turn for the worse or a situation becomes unacceptable (we will cover these in much more detail in Chapter 29).

The tripwire on this occasion was to set a daily alarm on Warren's phone, to remind him to ignore Roy. This was a simple message, as a tripwire needs to have a near-immediate impact, but it was only a temporary fix.

The bigger issue was Warren's relationship with his self. He faced a world full of 'Roys' each and every day – both physically and in the form of his trades. The front month crude contract and the DAX futures contract could become Roys, and he could not dismiss them in the same way he could sometimes do with 'office Roy'.

To be more successful as a trader, Warren needed to develop a better relationship with his self. This was a case where heavy lifting was required. I worked with Warren for more than three years. We spent many months looking at his trading, using the Performance Process Cycle as a way to unpick his behaviours at various stages of his process. He came to use the cycle as a navigational aid as he faced the market.

Though we made a steady improvement, I felt there was a lot more work Warren could do at the deeper level. But I am not a psychotherapist and must always be mindful not to tread in areas I am not qualified to go. I suggested to Warren that working with a psychotherapist I knew might be his next step.

The tripwire and the self-awareness building were helpful, but some issues require deeper work.

THE MARKET NEEDS YOU TO SLIP

I suggested for some time that Warren could benefit from having psychotherapy, but he remained reluctant. Then I told him that he was helping the market to do its work. This was a pivotal conversation. His reluctance to go to therapy was caused by his ego getting in his way again. I suggested that this was what the market wanted. It didn't want him to achieve his potential, and he was helping it.

One way to look at this is to consider your own participation in the markets as a giant poker game. As with poker, you can either lose by luck or you can lose because your ego undermines your ability to play well, causing you to make mistakes and eventually slide into a sub-optimal trader state and potentially a tilt state.

Once in a tilt state, there is a high probability that your money will become the market's. The market wants you to fall into a sub-optimal trader state and degrade into a tilt state. Your mental capital depletes first, your mental fortitude erodes and your physical capital follows.

That is what the market wants for you, hence the quote which starts this chapter.

The market has an agenda: it wants your money. To achieve this, it first convinces you that you can take money from it. The natural overconfidence of your ego in the face of a challenge helps ensure you take this bait. Then, when you try, it relies on your ego to undermine you and on you unravelling.

But this also creates openings for you. For the market to convince you that you can take its money, there must genuinely be a possibility of that outcome. You can do this by being skilled at the house approach or the player approach, or possibly by developing the even greater ability to play both.

If you can find a way to take its money and an approach where you can continually apply your mental capital, and you develop the mental fortitude not to unravel, you will play *your* game, not the market's game.

If you let the market inside your head, you will end up in a situation like Warren's.

When you say things like, "I hate the market", "screw the market", "this market is toying with me", "the market knows what I am doing", that is you allowing the market inside your head. Once there, it is occupying space rent-free. You are the one allowing it in and then making it worse by letting it stay there. One tip is to try to see the market as a natural force. Deny it personality and an ego of its own. When you do this, you can forcibly evict it from your head. Consider it like a mountain, an ocean, a valley – as a natural environment and something you must navigate, not something that has an agenda against you.

CHAPTER 11

The Power of Purpose

There is one quality which one must possess to win, and that is definiteness of purpose, the knowledge of what one wants, and a burning desire to possess it.

Napoleon Hill, author of Think and Grow Rich

"STEVE, I FEEL I have a competing purpose that's distracting me and influencing how I'm behaving. I need to talk to you about it."

I had barely had time to settle into my seat when the client, Suzanna, burst out with that sentence. Suzanna had been itching to share this with me, having reflected on it since our last session.

After calming her and composing myself, I asked her what she meant by a 'competing purpose'.

"I'm afraid to fail," she replied. "Or rather, I'm afraid of the damage failure will have on my reputation."

She stopped for a brief second, then continued. "It's this need to avoid failure which has become my purpose, and it's hijacking my trading."

"How is that manifesting in your work?" I asked her.

Responding in her rapid, combative style, she said, "I'm not following my usual behaviours and actions. I'm not doing what has always worked for me. I'm erratic, jumping around from idea to idea, reacting to every small move in the market, not following my process. I watch every tick, which is ridiculous, because my approach doesn't require me to watch every tick. I'm blaming others, firing off at others, angry at others, angry at myself."

"And who are these people judging you and your reputation?"

She went to answer me, but then stalled. She started to answer again, but then stalled again. Then she went silent – something I was not used to with this client.

I sat there in silence too, letting her think and reflect.

After a few moments she said (but slowly this time), "I'm not really sure."

Something had shifted.

Suzanna was a 25-year veteran of the markets who had just recently started at a new fund.

It had dawned on her, after a trip around the cycle in our previous session, that her purpose had shifted from making money to ensuring that her reputation would not be damaged. This fear of the loss of her reputation was the very thing that was affecting her trading and could ironically lead to reputational damage. Yet there was a paradox at work here. Suzanna's reputation was not at stake, because reputation is merely a figment of our ego's imagination. No one really cared about Suzanna's reputation other than her self.

This story requires some context. Suzanna had been bruised by her experience in her previous job. She was a classic house-approach trader, running long-short equity trades. However, for various reasons, things had not worked out at her last job.

There were nuances in Suzanna's approach and risk philosophy that ran counter to how things were done in her previous firm. These nuances had not seemed material when she joined, but became challenging as small issues soon developed into larger ones.

Suzanna resigned after two years at that firm, but she felt that if she had not done so she would have been released (that's the ego-acceptable way of saying 'fired').

Being fired hurts. It feels like rejection, the ego's number-one pet hate. There was a logical reason that her job had not worked out, which revolved around a mismatch between how she worked and how the firm worked. It was easy to see that this was not Suzanna's failure, but the ego does not deal in logic. Her ego was bruised, and though she quickly found a new job, she carried that bruising experience into it.

As Suzanna started in her new role, her ego was deeply agitated. It soon took control of the reins of her trading. In doing so, it hijacked her purpose. Once it had done this, it had broken into the 3 Ps of High Performance: her process and her ability to be present now became compromised.

Her work purpose was clear: she needed to use the capital the firm allocated to her to build a market-neutral portfolio of stocks she considered over-valued and undervalued. She would apply her knowledge, experience of various models and metrics, and her assessment of market sentiment connected to specific companies. Everything she would do in her work was aimed towards fulfilling her work purpose.

This helped her fulfil her broader purpose, which was to support and build a future for her family – to give them all the best chance in life. She also supported her parents, who were both disabled, and donated money to various philanthropic causes.

But, rocked by the bruising experience of her last job, Suzanna's ego took her on a different path in the new role. It was trying to fulfil an ego-led purpose: the restoration of her reputation.

THE POWER OF PURPOSE

One of the basic concepts which lies at the root of the Gestalt coaching philosophy which I subscribe too, and which influences many of the ideas in this book, is that 'awareness is healing'. This was the case with Suzanna. The realisation that her purpose had been hijacked, as a result of her recent experiences and circumstances, was of great comfort to her and was enough to bring her back to focusing on her core purpose.

In one session Suzanna stated explicitly what her purpose was, then wrote it down. With this simple act, she was able to become fully aligned with who she was – with her self. Her ego became calm and she let go of the negative ego baggage from her previous experience.

On reflection, we realised that Suzanna had not checked in with her purpose when she started her new role. She had not focused on her purpose or aligned her self with her purpose. She had bypassed the entire Being Phase of the cycle, because she had not got closure on her last experience. She came into her new role wanting to prove a point.

The first part of every cycle is about visiting your purpose – what it is you are seeking to do – to ensure that what follows is connected to your purpose and that your purpose doesn't drift or morph into alternative purposes.

Cycles work on various levels. We can have micro-cycles, which represent a single trading decision, or larger cycles representing a month's worth of trades or which relate to a different aspect of your life altogether. The larger cycles are often the more challenging ones because they corrupt the lower-level ones.

A WHOLESOME PURPOSE

Every cycle should start with a wholesome purpose aligned with who you are and what you want to achieve. A purpose is 'wholesome' if it brings your ego along with you rather than being led by it. You need to work with your ego, not fight it. This wholesome purpose is your core purpose.

An ego-led purpose that aims to impact how you appear to others is not a wholesome purpose.

The money question often pops up when purpose is discussed. Many people go into trading because they dream of being rich, but it is what is behind that motive that matters.

"I want to be rich, own fast cars and expensive watches, and make other people jealous," is clearly an ego-led purpose. It will probably go the same way as most ego-led purposes.

"I want money to attain financial independence, to build a future for my family, to make sure my investors are rewarded for their loyalty, to have the ability to help and positively influence others." This is an example of a wholesome purpose.

A wholesome purpose is something your core self could get behind. An ego-led purpose sees you being owned by the desire to impress others.

My work as a coach has alerted me to how much energy people devote to worrying about what others think about them, and how destructive this behaviour is. *But if you are thinking this way, so is everyone else.* So, riddle me this: how can they be thinking about you, when they are too busy worrying what you and others think of them?

Reflecting on this can be incredibly liberating and powerful.

I co-host the AlphaMind Podcast with my colleague Mark Randall. It explores many of the topics and themes discussed in this book. We were very fortunate to have the wonderful Morgan Housel, author of the bestselling book *The Psychology of Money,* as a guest a couple of year ago.

In our interview Morgan talked about what he calls 'the man in the car paradox'. It refers to a time in his life when he was working as a valet attendant at a local restaurant. The restaurant's customers would pull up in some of the most desirable cars on the planet. They would toss him the keys, and it was his job to park these Ferraris, Lamborghinis, Porsches and Bentleys.

It occurred to Morgan that, while he paid great attention to the cars, he barely noticed the people driving them. As he put it: "You rarely think, 'Wow, that guy driving that car is cool'. Instead, you think, 'Wow, if I had that car people would think I'm cool'."

This is how people think. This is the paradox.

People do not notice the man in the car. Instead they see the car, then they think "I want to have that car so that people can notice me as 'the man in the car'."

As Morgan points out, people are often benchmarking themselves against their peers through their own desire to be liked and admired. Or rather, their ego is.

As humans, we are all driven by social influence on some level. As much as we like to feel we are engaging in rational choices born of logic and intellect, our actions are being set by the cultural norms of the society around us, the ecosystems we exist within and the attitudes and behaviours of the groups we consciously and subconsciously subscribe to.

We have a need to be respected and admired by others, particular our peers. This exerts an invisible gravitational pull on our behaviours, attitudes, and actions – in ways we are rarely conscious of.

This gravitational pull directs both our actions and our avoidance actions. The avoidance actions may even have a stronger influence on us due to our natural loss aversion, a phenomenon whereby people feel more pain (typically more than twice as much) from losing something than the pleasure from gaining something of equal value.

Thus, we unconsciously act in ways which aim to keep us safe from disapproval, disrespect, ridicule, contempt, humiliation, shame and the ultimate sanction: being rejected by peers and ejected from a community we belong to.

YOUR TRADING PURPOSE

Your trading purpose should enable your core purpose to be achieved. To effectively achieve this your trading purpose must be carefully designed to align with the nature of your trading work, available resources, and other important considerations, such as who you are trading for and whether you work for a buy-side or sell-side firm.

Some examples of a trading purpose include:

- An FX market-maker working for a bank might have the purpose of supporting the bank to make markets in the currency franchise they have responsibility for, including pricing to their clients and customers. They have to do this in a way which enables them to generate a profit, support volume turnover and sales functions, and work within risk parameters.

- An energy trader working for a producer may have a similar purpose, but it might specify the management of energy assets and fulfilment and delivery of physical energy products in addition to trading profitability and managing risk prudently.

- A buy-side trader's purpose would be different. They do not have a franchise or physical business function. Their purpose might be to use capital allocated to them and then to either trade it using leverage or invest it in tradable assets, with a view to generating a sufficient return on that capital in line with a mandate given to them by the business, acting within specific risk parameters.

- A retail trader's purpose would be different again. Their purpose is to trade their money and capital, using electronic platforms and leverage offered to them by a broker, to trade profitably and generate an income for themselves, while building their capital and being careful not to deplete their 'limited' trading capital.

THE WAY (THE WHAT AND THE HOW)

Your plan for achieving your purpose – how you will play your outer game – defines the structure of your playbook.

A playbook can be thought of as both a mission statement and a set of rules, guidelines, strategies and tactics which you will apply in your trading. It can also be used as a place to 'write' down or state your bargain with your self.

Everything that you do in your process should be aligned in some way to your playbook.

The playbook should not be fixed. You can adapt and evolve it over time. If you do write it down, it is best not to go into too much detail. This will allow for evolution and adaptation, and prevent you becoming too constrained.

You can have multiple playbooks. A client of mine has one playbook for when the markets he trades are in a clear bullish phase, one for a bearish phase and another for sideways markets. Another client reviews his playbook regularly and adjusts it to the underlying environment of the markets. Yet another client has an active playbook and a passive playbook, the latter being for periods when he wants to pull back from the market. Though I never defined my playbook fully in writing, it manifested in the notes I made in my journals over the years, and I had a list of rules and guidelines I adhered to which were always included in the front of my trading journals.

One client has created what he jokingly calls his 'coma book'. If he ever goes into a coma, then comes out with his memory wiped, it's a reminder to him of all the things he does and why.

GOAL-SETTING

As I set out to write this part of the chapter on goals and goal-setting, I find myself at slight odds with myself, and having contradictory thoughts.

It is because I am uncomfortable with goals and dislike the way most people go about goal-setting. Do not misunderstand me, I am not against goals; quite the opposite, we need them as objectives which motivate us. My issue is how goals are set.

Goals should come from your purpose, adhere to your purpose and should respect reality. Often people set goals with no respect to reality or to their core (wholesome) purpose. If anything, they stem from ego-led desires.

Suzanna was working towards goals set by her ego-led need to restore her reputation. This was very similar to Kyle's story in Chapter 3.

So much performance destruction results from goals that are misaligned with purpose. This is as true for a bank setting goals for its traders as for a new trader setting a goal which is a fantasy they aspire too.

Goals should be outcomes you aspire to. They should emerge from your purpose; they should never lead your purpose. They should however seek to take you to the edge of your comfort zone and potentially beyond. Comfort zones are nice places, but very little grows there.

CHAPTER 12

The Trader's Bargain With Their Self

The most important negotiation in your life is 'getting to yes' with yourself. When you learn to do that, you start winning at everything else.

Erica Ariel Fox, author of Winning From Within

IN THE SUMMER of 2011, I placed a short AUDUSD FX trade. I was no longer a professional trader at that point, but I still traded through a private account. I had sold AUDUSD at close to 1.1000, with a view that it might be due for a correction back towards 1.0000. The stop I placed on this trade was above 1.1100.

My reasoning for the trade was that the AUDUSD had been in a strong bull market, rallying from a low of 0.9700 a few months earlier, and from near 0.8000 over the previous year. From a fundamental perspective, I felt the strength of the AUDUSD was unsustainable at these levels. Technically, the upside momentum was waning, and the spot FX rate was struggling to break through a high from a few weeks earlier.

On the evening of the day I placed the trade, I had a quick glance at my phone; it had rallied 50 ticks since the London markets had closed. I had a gut reaction. "What the hell?" I thought. Not much normally happens in AUDUSD after hours. My ego's instant response was: "Close the trade, Steve!" I was tired, it had been a long day, and I did not have much energy left to fight my ego.

I had my trade account open on my phone ready to close the position. It was at that point I recalled my psychological contract – which is the bargain I had made with my self – one aspect of which states "I accept losses as the price of winning." I reminded myself that there was a reason I had placed the stop on the trade where it was. As far as I could see, that reason had not changed, therefore I should let the trade be.

The next day the market was lower again, and for a few days the trade remained in a narrow range near 1.1000. Then the following week it broke lower, and within two weeks it had sold off sharply, hitting 1.0000.

I got enormous personal satisfaction from this trade.

The bargain I made with myself was contained in my psychological contract. My psychological contract was not something I explicitly wrote out, but it came together as a result of many experiences over many years and was more implicit than explicit.

As part of the bargain I made with myself, I would accept trading losses when they happened, whether they were revaluation losses on an open position, or actual losses cemented when I closed out a trade. This bargain made it both easier to sit with losing trades and to place trades, knowing that they had a strong possibility of being losses. Recall that my method was a classic player approach, whereby I would lose far more often that I would win, but when a trade won, typically it would win larger size profits than the many collective losses.

To help remind me of this bargain I made with myself, I developed a mantra – 'Learn to love your losses'. The full meaning of which was 'Learn to love your losses since without them you will never win.'

Reminding myself of this mantra regularly, particularly in cases such as this AUDUSD FX situation, would allow me to recall my bargain with myself, and helped quieten my agitated ego rather than allow it into my process.

THE TRADER'S BARGAIN AND THE TWO APPROACHES

The nature of a trader's bargain will be very different depending on their dominant philosophical approach to trading. The bargain a trader taking the player approach strikes will be very different to the one a house-approach trader makes.

Whichever approach you use, the bargain aims to help you to become aligned with your self in pursuit of your purpose. Since the quality of the trader's relationship with their self is the key to successful trading, this bargain is central to your success. You have probably already struck some form of bargain, but at this point it is 'implicit' only.

The following sections outline the main aspects a trader's bargain with their self should consider, in reference to each of the two approaches.

THE PLAYER-APPROACH BARGAIN

In general, traders who approach the market with a player-approach mentality intrinsically understand that they have to accept periods of underperformance, missed opportunities, and unpredictable returns in exchange for the potential to generate significant profits over time. However, this approach can vary substantially between individuals. For instance, traders operating with a short-term focus or in a high-liquidity environment may tailor their approach to reflect the specific factors impacting their trades, such as market volatility or unique timeframes.

An optimal trader state using the player-approach will enable the trader to use their capital appropriately and to leverage it wisely when favourable setups occur. They can then optimise their upside when conditions are right.

The bargain should be written in a way that helps keep the trader in an optimal trader state and enables them to work in a way which helps them achieve their purpose, while staying present to their process.

There should be some non-negotiables for all player-approach traders, including respect their risk and money-management rules, and those of their stakeholders, so they can manage their inevitable drawdowns and not overexpose their downside.

As part of the trader's bargain, they also need to emphasise elements which help them manage their personal state. One example of this could be to emphasise the importance for a player-approach trader of creating distance from the noise of the market and the internal clutter in their head, such that they can make clear and coherent assessments that facilitate the crafting and application of sound strategies and plans, yet, at the same time, the trader should ensure they stay close enough to the noise of the markets, so they can gain the valuable insights this brings.

This is a key feature of the challenge player-approach traders need to focus on: the ability to maintain their distance from the noise – to see the bigger picture with objectivity – while staying on-top of the detail so they can get close-up and dirty with the terrain, so as to understand what is happening down there.

The player-approach trader needs to carefully manage their psychology, particulary during barren spells and drawdowns. They need to work in situations and contexts that are supportive and conducive to their working approach.

They also need to maintain personal balance with the external world and with those who matter to them, lest the external world rebound and unbalance them. They should be mindful of the impact their mood may have on those close to them, which can rebound on them and affect their trading, let alone the impact mood has directly on themselves and their trading.

If you apply the player approach, you will need to consider how best to manage these elements as a feature of your playbook. Take time-outs and regular breaks, engage in activities which help restore personal balance and try to make space and time for those who matter most to you.

THE HOUSE-APPROACH BARGAIN

The typical house-approach trader's bargain may stress that they should be paid and rewarded, often regularly, by monetising the fine edge the market offers them. They should be aware that while this, in theory at least, makes the house approach psychologically less challenging, it requires the taking of significant amounts of risk, and relies on high levels of intensity, hard work, and commitment which can erode away at their physical and mental well-being.

By seeking to get into an optimal trader state, the house-approach trader will seek to regularly deploy risk, capital and leverage skilfully to capture the endowments of their franchise, system, situation or context, while being careful to honour their risk parameters.

House-approach traders must also be aware of the hidden risks in their approach – the sting in the fat-tail. This can and does see periodic large drawdowns and may even have the potential for 'risk-of-ruin' – an irrecoverable loss of capital.

House-approach methods require traders to develop the ability to remain constantly vigilant and to cultivate the intuitive skills which foster 'proactive defensiveness'. They should acquire the ability to perform in the face of adversity, in order to generate income in a consistent and sustainable manner. However, they have to be mindful that this exposes them occasionally to outsize drawdowns. This is to be expected, rather than being a flaw or a failure. However, they only need to get caught once by the steamroller for it to be 'game over'.

Private and retail house-approach traders do not have the advantage of external risk parameters, or a risk department or managerial oversight. They therefore need to create a structure for themselves which protects them from being overexposed to the dreaded margin call.

A key challenge house-approach traders need to focus on is developing the ability to get close-up and dirty in the mud of the terrain, and yet retain enough distance to see themselves and the market with enough objectivity to encompass the bigger picture. Though this sounds similar to one of the challenges of the player-approach trader, the emphasis is different, since proximity to market liquidity is a priority for the house-approach trader.

A house-approach trader who can create a bargain with themselves, and then honour this bargain potentially can thrive and create a sustainable trading practice, however the house-approach trader should be conscious that setbacks will happen. They should hold it in their mind that these tend to be temporary and that over time the systems should deliver. They should, however, continue to keep an eye on evolving and developing their system. Most systems need adaptation over time as market conditions evolve.

They should also be mindful that since their approach is akin to picking up pennies in front of a steamroller, they need to be willing to sacrifice some upside to protect themselves against a terminal outcome. Even the greatest house-approach trader of them all, Jim Simons, reportedly overrode their system to avoid a margin call, during a period known as the quant quake in 2007. "Our job is to survive" Simons said, "If we're wrong, we can always add [positions] later."[2]

When following the house approach, the situation you work in should be supportive and provide the right context and environmental conditions for this type of trading. The house approach is high energy, and your mental capital will deplete rapidly throughout the day. This depletion will impact your mood and energy levels. You should be mindful of your impact on those who matter to you, and make space and time for them. You should also manage your self carefully, so that you can be at your physical and mental best. This is possibly a higher priority for the house-approach trader, due to the higher intensity usually involved with this approach.

CHAPTER 13

Detached Curiosity

I am better off than he is, for he knows nothing, and thinks that he knows. I neither know nor think that I know.

Socrates, philosopher

A S MENTIONED EARLIER in this book, the ability to practice detached curiosity is crucial. This is a subtle yet powerful behaviour that I have observed while working with exceptional traders. Interestingly, they are often not even aware of it, as it has become second nature to them. However, I have come to realise that this is one of those 'stealth behaviours' that differentiates those who excel at trading and investing from the rest of the field.

Detached curiosity is a non-ego state in which you are purposely indifferent. You observe and notice, and you deliberately put yourself in a position of not-knowing, so that, ironically, *you can know more*. You allow yourself to ask questions without attachment to what these questions imply about you, and you carefully consider your responses rather than rushing to respond.

One time I was listening to one of my favourite podcasts, The Jolly Swagman. The host, Joseph Walker, was presenting yet another brilliant and thought-provoking interview with a guest. Joseph's model is to state a thesis or proposition and then put it to his guest.

On this occasion, after Joseph's opening thesis, his guest responded with, "Let me think my way into this."

Seven little powerful words: "Let me think my way into this." I thought this phrase would be common, so I googled it. Not one single search result came up. By comparison, when I randomly typed some letters on my keyboard – creating the word 'hughuged' – and ran a search for this, I got 286 results.

I can make up a meaningless word on Google and get results, yet not one result for the phrase "Let me think my way into this" or even for its slight modification, "Let me think my way into that."

"Let me think my way into this" was a momentary pause which distanced the guest in that moment from his ego. He was not indifferent to the question, but he did display creative indifference. That is to say, he wanted to ensure he understood it, thought about it, and responded to it with creativity, coherence and clarity.

Those I meet who excel in trading, investing and management often display this ability to exercise detached curiosity. For a few seconds, they can be 'creatively indifferent'.

DETACHED CURIOSITY AND THE WILLINGNESS TO BE VULNERABLE

People who can work with and apply detached curiosity have an edge. The player-approach trader is able to go beyond and beneath the data, getting a little closer to the terrain without getting lost in it. The house-approach trader is able to operate deep in the terrain and yet not get bogged down in it; they can still glimpse the bigger picture.

I believe that when traders operate in the market, they are operating at three levels. The first level is about seeing, observing and sensing. The second level is having a primary sense of what this means. This is where the ego comes in; it wants to *know* what the implication is, and it starts constructing a story, image, or narrative. The third level is truly being aware of what this means, and then being able to react appropriately to it. It requires going deeper into the news, data, information and having a deeper sense of what it implies.

When the ego comes in, it can be difficult to reach the third level. If you are able to suspend your ego, then step back from immediate judgement, you have more chance of reaching the third level. This is where a trader has an edge, they can have a more rounded or deeper understanding of what the news and the market movements imply in the moment.

Detached curiosity is a way of reaching this third level. Going deep, and exercising detached curiosity while immersed in the markets, enables you to get a clearer understanding of the bigger picture and the terrain. It allows you to see further and wider. You will not merely see matters through your own lens but get a glimpse of the world through the lens of others.

When Stanley Druckenmillar and George Soros assessed the disagreement between the UK government and the Bundesbank, they were operating at the third level, which allowed them to update their assessment of the unfolding situation with greater clarity. When the head of trading at the bank sensed all was not right with the SNB's commitment to the Swiss franc peg with the Euro, he was operating at the third level. They were player-approach traders, but when the head of trading's views on the Swiss Franc were disseminated amongst the FX traders, who were house-approach traders, they were immediately aware of what this implied for them. They reacted favourably to the situation, while the rest of the market froze.

While exercising detached curiosity, you are not expressing judgement, agreeing or disagreeing, but are merely observing and noticing. You are adopting a state of not-knowing. This requires a commitment to being vulnerable, which may upset both your ego and other people's fragile egos. But, you must be willing to say, "I don't know the answer. I don't understand the issue. I am clueless."

That is what the great traders, leaders and managers do.

One manager, who was promoted from a trading role to become the head of a large business, told me that he was terrified about stepping into the role. He said he did not know the work or jobs of many people he would be managing and sensed a lot of dissatisfaction with his promotion from those who would be reporting to him.

When we discussed this, he thought that he should know all about their jobs. I suggested that this was impossible, and that his job was to manage and lead them, not to know everything they do.

We concluded that he would do better admitting to them that he did not know. He could then admit that he would be relying on them to work with him and help him.

After that, he called his various teams together for a first meeting, then put himself out there. He said to them that he did not know most of their jobs, the minutiae of their work or the intricacies of their roles. He said he would not pretend to know and would rely on them partnering with him to keep him informed. In return he offered to lead them to the best of his ability.

In that moment he felt all the opposition to his promotion evaporate.

He formed a great partnership with the leaders of the various teams over the months and years that followed. He kept himself open and vulnerable, and as a result came to know more than he could ever have known had he pretended that he knew.

BEING VULNERABLE MEANS BEING WILLING TO ASK FOR HELP

In the hit TV series *Billions*, about fictional hedge fund billionaire Bobby 'Axe' Axelrod, there is a scene where performance coach Wendy Rhoades is giving a talk to an audience of hedge fund portfolio managers. In that talk she tells the gathering that in their minds, "The thought that someone might know you need help is worse than not getting the help you need."

I had to pause at this point because that was once me, and it is most people I have met in the trading business, with very few exceptions. But often those exceptions have the best results. They are not afraid to ask for help, they relish it.

A few years back, I had the privilege of working alongside a remarkable trader who was a senior portfolio manager at a hedge fund. When I questioned him about why he sought out coaching, he responded, "I love being helped. It is when I stop asking for help that I get into trouble."

I will admit that I was once one of those people who Wendy Rhoades was talking about. The thought that others might know I need help or sought help, was worse in my mind than not getting the help I needed.

I no longer think that way, and I am able to write from my current perspective due to the journey I have been on. This journey started with me as a trader working with an amazing coach called Peter Burditt.

I started working with Peter in the year 2000, almost a decade and a half into my trading career. The opportunity to do so occurred as a result of fortunate circumstances. This proved to be the most pivotal event of my trading career, yet it was an opportunity I, inspired by my ego, very nearly spurned.

The opportunity occurred because our new head of trading at Commerzbank, where I worked, was keen to bring Peter in to work with his traders. He, himself, had been coached by Peter at his previous bank.

The new head of trading approached me to ask if I would work in a trial programme funded by the bank.

Ideally, my response should have been something along the lines of "Let me think my way into that," followed a short time later by, "Yes, that could be of huge benefit to me." But instead my response was, "I don't need a coach, there's nothing wrong with me."

Or, to paraphrase Wendy Rhoades, the idea that others might know I might need help was a barrier I was not prepared to cross.

That was my ego intervening, taking control. The ego saw the need for help as a threat to my self-image, which it had carefully crafted.

This was to be a pivotal moment for me.

At that point in time, my career was hitting the rocks. I was barely hanging on. What I needed was help, but my ego was stopping me getting it.

I got fortunate. Our new head of trading was nothing if not persistent. He came back later that day and subtly twisted my arm.

I can credit my far stronger performance as a trader over the next ten years to that pivotal moment.

It is not lost on me, how often I have been invited into prop firms, hedge funds and investment banks to give talks about my work to groups of traders and portfolio managers. What I see on the faces of the attendees is: "I don't need help, there is nothing wrong with me."

In one example I was asked to talk to a group of new portfolio managers and analysts at a hedge fund in Hong Kong. The meeting was arranged for me to explain to them the work I do, and they could then opt to take advantage of my services as a coach. That was a hell of a way to fly me out for a 60-minute meeting.

There were 20 new junior portfolio managers and analysts in the meeting. I could sense, from the looks on their faces and their body language, that this was not going to be a successful trip. Not one of the attendees so much as emailed or called me after to inquire about the coaching.

But two weeks later I got a call from a new portfolio manager who had been due to be at the meeting but had been on vacation. She assumed that all the attendees were going to rush to participate and wanted to get ahead of them in my diary. She was the only one who followed up.

Within two years that new portfolio manager was one of the few members of that group who was still at the fund. She had practised detached curiosity with regard to the coaching. Six years later she is still there and now oversees their Asian business.

There have been a handful of people, like this trader, who over the years have bucked this "I don't need help" trend. In nearly all cases, they were either achieving great things or went on to achieve great things.

Another example of this occurred when I gave a talk to a large group of prop traders at a firm in London. No one from that meeting responded, but then one prop trader who was not there but had heard about it reached out to me. His name was Daljit Dhaliwal. If you have read Jack D. Schwager's *Unknown Market Wizards* (Harriman House, 2020), you will have read about Daljit.

Like the portfolio manager just mentioned, Daljit was not afraid to exercise detached curiosity and ask for help. Quite the opposite. He had been an avid follower of another Market Wizard, Peter Brandt. When he heard Peter was attending a conference in Europe, he made sure he attended, then met and spoke with him.

Daljit also ensured he won a charity auction which was offering lunch in New York with hedge fund legend Ray Dalio as a prize. Daljit had been heavily influenced by Dalio's principles, and the chance to go deeper – to the third level – with Dalio, was not something he was going to pass up.

I spent almost four years working with Daljit. He is one of the most incredible traders I have come across. He displays and practises detached curiosity in everything he does.

Two of Daljit's colleagues, Amrit Sall and Richard Bargh, both exceptional traders, were also willing to embrace being helped and participated in the coaching. Both also featured in *Unknown Market Wizards*. Both practise detached curiosity in their trading.

When I work with people such as these, I do not credit the coaching with their success. I am sure it proved useful and beneficial, but it is the fact that they were willing to be vulnerable and open to being helped that lies behind their success. Success for these people was highly probable because they practised detached curiosity in their lives and their work.

CHAPTER 14

Presence – Your True Self

Knowing your self is the beginning of all wisdom.

Aristotle, philosopher

THE EGO IS a simple, 'virtual' organism. It is simply trying to fulfil what it perceives as its duty to you. You have a choice: you can either try to work with your ego, or you can try to fight it. The purpose of the 3Ps of High Performance is to help you work *with* it. Successful application of and adherence to the 3Ps can keep the ego calm.

The toughest of the 3Ps to adhere to is 'presence'. The first two Ps, purpose and process, are largely transactional. However, when it comes to being present you are simply too close to your self to be able to act transactionally. And yet the very best traders are able to be fully present. It is as if this kind of trader has the ability to stand apart from their self, to see their self at a distance.

I have heard such traders describe moments in which time momentarily seemed to stand still, and they thought, "What does this moment require me to do?" Then, when they had worked it out, they were ready to go. That is being completely present.

This incredible ability is a feature of all great performers. It is what distinguishes Lionel Messi, Novak Djokovic, Michael Jordan and the other greats of the performance world from their competitors.

In the Netflix docuseries about the Chicago Bulls of the 1990s, *The Last Dance*, sportswriter Mark Vancil said of Michael Jordan:

> His gift was not that he could jump high, run fast, shoot a basketball. His gift was that he was completely present, and that was the separator. He didn't allow what he couldn't control to get inside his head. He would say, "Why would I think about missing a shot I haven't taken yet?"

The defining feature of Michael Jordan, according to Vancil, was his ability to be completely present.

Presence in high performers comes from their mastery of the self and the quality of their relationship with the self. No one owns them; instead they own everything they do.

My all-time sports hero, Muhammad Ali, is another of these greats. In his book *The Winner's Bible* (HarperCollins, 2013), cognitive neuroscientist Dr Kerry Spackman captures an example of Ali's mastery of self.

The story revolves around the most famous boxing match in history, 'The Rumble in the Jungle', which took place in Zaire (now the Democratic Republic of the Congo) in 1974.

The fight involved Ali and incumbent world champion George Foreman in a battle for the heavyweight championship of the world. Foreman was considered almost unbeatable. He was undefeated and had beaten the only two boxers to have defeated Ali, demolishing them both inside two rounds. He was a fearsome, muscular specimen of a boxer with the cold, dead eyes of an assassin.

Foreman was in his prime, whereas Ali, seven years Foreman's senior, was considered past his best. Ali was very much the underdog. Some even feared for his life as he went into the ring with Foreman.

Foreman was a man-mountain with a thundering punch. But on the night, in a fight that has gone down in sporting folklore, Ali overturned the odds to defeat him.

What is less well known is a moment that occurred during the pre-fight sparring sessions in the weeks leading up to the fight, which may have been pivotal to the outcome that night.

Sparring sessions saw top-quality fighters flown in for boxers to practise with ahead of a fight. Afterwards, the boxers and their camp (the coaches, trainers and managers) would sit down with the sparring partner and seek feedback from them.

Sparring partners were usually keen to avoid upsetting the boxers and their camps. However, one of Ali's partners was a bit more frank than usual. He told Ali and his camp that Foreman was going to flatten Ali. He said, "He's too big and he's too strong. He'll take your punches no problem and then punish you. You just aren't powerful enough to hurt him."

Ali's camp were furious, feeling that this boxer's candidness was likely to disturb Ali's mindset and undermine his confidence. They shut him down and told him to get on his way. They were reacting at the second level of information.

Ali, however, had other ideas. Acting at the third level of information, he welcomed the feedback and sensed there was something in what the sparring partner was saying.. He told his manager, "Double his salary. He stays until he tells me when I'm going to beat George."

In that moment, Ali accepted his vulnerability. He was comfortable enough in his relationship with his self that he could accept he was not perfect. He was thus willing to hear painful feedback. He sensed the sparring partner was right: he could not possibly go toe-to-toe with Foreman.

That was Ali being completely present.

Ali started working on a new approach. He knew that Foreman had not experienced long fights – rarely did he need to go beyond five rounds.

Given the heat and humidity of the jungle, Foreman's energy would become sapped as the fight wore on. Ali was masterful at defence – he could take punches and had exceptional ring craft which drew much of the power from his opponent. He could also throw sharp, stinging punches. Boxers often talked about not seeing Ali's punches coming until after he had hit them.

Ali and his camp settled on a strategy which would draw Foreman's strength and then allow for a blistering counter. They knew that Foreman's camp would probably guess that Ali would try a ploy like this, so they needed a ruse. The plan was to surprise Foreman by coming out fighting in the first round, then retreat to the ropes for the subsequent rounds. Here Ali would absorb Foreman's punches and sap his strength while preserving his own. This became known as the 'rope-a-dope' strategy.

However, the preparation was not just about strategy. Ali was going to face a serious beating for much of the fight, so he trained himself for this. Over the next few weeks, the sparring focused almost exclusively on defence. Massive sparring partners were told to pin Ali back on the ropes and lash out at him, working aggressively on his midsection. Here Ali could work on priming his reflexes for the conditions he would face in the fight.

During the fight Foreman did everything asked of him. His manager, Dick Sadler, said, "Everything we planned to do, cutting the ring, overpowering Ali, going after him, was designed to put him on the ropes." What they had not banked on was that this was exactly what Ali had planned for. They thought Foreman was owning Ali when all along Ali was owning Foreman.

As the fight continued, and Foreman's trademark haymaker punches were failing to land, Ali grew in confidence. He started taunting Foreman. "Is that all you got, George?" he said. By the eighth round, Foreman's strength was dissipating fast. "Man! This is the wrong place to get tired!" Ali said to him. Then Ali hit him with a combination that caused Foreman to stagger. He followed this with a hard right to the head. Foreman went down and was out for the count.

This result was possible because Ali was present and willing to be vulnerable at a key moment. He was not desensitised to negative feedback. His ego was relegated to the background. It was just him and his true self.

HEEDING THE MIRROR

During a recent series of workshops, my colleague Mark Randall (who also co-hosts the AlphaMind Podcast with me) was approached by an attendee who expressed their gratitude for Mark's helping them to become a better trader. Mark replied, "We're not working on making you a better trader, but a better you – so you can be a better trader." This captures the essence of the mental game. Trading is not that hard, but bringing the best version of your self to the game is.

Mastering your self requires getting to know your self – to fully understand your self. The ego often conspires to get in the way of us being able to do this. It fears that revealing the true self – the self it knew as a child – will undermine you. This is what was happening to Warren in Chapter 10, which made it difficult for me to help him.

In life we construct self-images, helped by the ego. This is the ego doing its job of ensuring we are accepted. This is the image of our self that it wants to project to the world.

These self-images are rarely our true selves, but instead are ego-adapted versions. We all do this to some degree. This is not a bug in how we function, but a feature.

The more alignment there is between our self-images and our true selves, the easier it is to be authentic and to bring our true selves to the moment. The mirrors which life holds up to us enable us to see our true selves. When we are comfortable in who we are, we are more comfortable heeding the reflection. When we are not comfortable with our true selves, we stop looking in mirrors and heeding the feedback they give to us.

Muhammed Ali was not afraid of what his mirror reflected; he was open to listening. If he had not been, it is quite possible The Rumble in the Jungle would not have gone the way it did.

My own pivotal moment occurred when Peter Burditt held up a virtual mirror to me during coaching.

For the first time, I had a chance to see my real self, warts and all; not the idealised version of myself that my ego wanted me to see.

Your real self is infinitely more powerful than that self-image. Your self-image is a fake version of you. It is like a film set or a Potemkin village. From a distance it looks real and genuine. It can fool other people, but there is nothing behind it.

Your real self is comfortable getting to the third level of information, it is your ego-created self-image which gets in the way.

I have had many great teachers, mentors and guides on my journey as a coach – Peter being one of them. Another is the fantastic coach Maria Iliffe-Wood, who is ironically my book coach, advising and guiding me on the writing of this book.

I first met Maria when she ran a local community of coaches, the Welwyn Co-Coaching forum, in my area. As a coach, Maria put a lot of emphasis on helping people and coaches become more present and developing their presence. She has written extensively on these themes.

In one meeting, Maria introduced a wonderful metaphor in which she described everyone as possessing a diamond at their core. The diamond represents that person's true potential and their inner wisdom. It is that diamond which sits at the centre of that person's true, authentic and powerful self.

The realities of life cause us to cover that diamond up. Each coping mechanism we develop, starting in childhood, acts like a layer of varnish painted over that diamond. With each layer, the diamond sparkles less and less, until eventually it is no longer visible. Yet the diamond remains there, always present, always with the potential to sparkle like the most brilliant gem. You can only ever access that diamond by being your true self.

The coaching work I did with Peter enabled me to look in the mirror and see the true me, my real self, and to start connecting with it. That self has power within it and substance behind it. That was the version of myself I needed to bring to the table in my work.

KNOWING YOUR SELF IS THE BEGINNING OF ALL WISDOM

In trading we can all acquire knowledge, learn about the fundamentals, the technicals, the history of the markets. We can be a walking encyclopaedia of knowledge and have a list of qualifications as long as our arm. But until you truly know your self, you will never achieve your full potential.

This is what Aristotle meant when he said, "Knowing your self is the beginning of all wisdom."

My coaching with Peter started to reveal my self to me. I recall in one coaching session, after reviewing the results of a psychometric test, Peter said, "I am surprised you are a trader considering how analytical you are."

I found this puzzling. "Surely that's why I'm right for trading!" I thought. Then I started pondering this. I was indeed very strong on analysis; it helped me find many great trading ideas. I would delve deep below the surface of the markets, looking for clues like a financial market Colombo, trying to solve a murder which had occurred in the Bund market.

But, as I reflected, it occurred to me that often my ability would stop there. I was applying myself to finding value but struggled to monetise that value. I was a living embodiment of Warren Buffett's Noah rule: "Predicting rain doesn't count, building arks does." I predicted rain but was a poor builder of arks.

I realised that I had better start improving my ark-building skills. That was the new puzzle I had to work on. To do that, I had to engage markets at the third level.

Until then, my ego had stopped me reaching the third level, where I could understand what was happening in the moment and then act on it.

My inability to engage at the third level was holding me back. To access this level, I had to be willing to be vulnerable. But my ego would not allow it. This meant I sought 'safe risk' (somewhat of an oxymoron), as well as 'low risk' or 'no risk'. My ego would then excuse the underperformance which resulted by blaming others. If I could find fault in the world around me, my own self-image remained safe; no one would discover it was a fake – or so I thought.

I blamed the management, the bank, the bank's culture, the constant turnover at the bank, the sales desk, the systems. Sometimes the blame went beyond the bank: the algorithms, the brokers, the central banks, the analysts, the economists.

It is possible that some of that blame was warranted. But that is not an excuse; those factors were just part of the environment I worked in. I could always have changed jobs. But here I was safe, I was in my comfort zone. In your comfort zone, nothing grows.

If I had continued down that path, I am pretty sure my trading career would have hit the rocks. It was already bumping up against them.

As a result of this awakening, which started with coaching, I began to focus on what I had to do to win. I was now present to the task in hand, not to the preservation of my self-image.

Knowing your self is the start. This is the 'you' that you must take into the trade.

CHAPTER 15

Effective Journalling

I don't journal to 'be productive'. I don't do it to find great ideas or to put down prose I can later publish. The pages aren't intended for anyone but me. It's the most cost-effective therapy I've ever found.

Tim Ferriss, author and podcaster

I N AN EPISODE of the Chat With Traders podcast, Tom Dante (known on social media as Trader Dante) tells a story of a time when he was working in a prop trading firm.

There were a couple of large aggressive prop traders at the firm who could regularly produce significant income. One of these traders had a hugely successful day, and the buzz in the trading room was about how much money this trader had made.

At the end of the day, Tom left the office to have a few drinks with colleagues, then headed home. When he got home, he realised he had left his key in the office. He headed back to fetch the key, arriving at about 9.30pm.

All the office lights were out except for one at the back, where Tom could see someone quietly working away. He walked over and, to his surprise, it was the trader who had had a huge day. He was filling out his journal, reviewing his trades and actions through that day, and making his plans for the next.

Tom had assumed that he would be out celebrating in a bar or a pub, but instead he was filling out his journal. This is what great traders do. They do exceptional things. They go that extra mile often and regularly.

Journalling is one of the practices many exceptional traders follow. They also review trades and assess their personal performance.

There are few things more valuable for a trader than journalling. Journals are cheap, easy to use and simple to keep. Yet few people use them or fully utilise them in ways they benefit from.

The objective of a well-maintained trader's journal, used in a constructive and diligent manner, is to power one's trading. Journalling can achieve this in various ways, including providing a space to write out your playbook, but I feel it is most helpful in enabling you to build a mirror.

By helping you build a mirror, a journal becomes a focus for continual learning and development, as well as true self-reflection.

Trading is you against the market, and you against your ego. The odds of winning these twin battles separately are long enough – winning them together is even harder. But victory is possible. The markets offer an opportunity for you to win, but you need every bit of help you can muster. Keeping a journal is one way you can help your self.

3-3-1 FRAMEWORK – A SIMPLIFIED JOURNALLING APPROACH

Journalling is a great tool for reflection, self-awareness and self-improvement. The problem is most people struggle to motivate themselves to do the journalling. Journalling tends to be put in that category of "I'll do it tomorrow." Unfortunately, we know what happens to most things in that category.

Therefore, even though people recognise the positive impacts of journalling, many neglect to do it, or do it ineffectively, consequently missing out on its vast potential for helping them improve as traders.

The 3-3-1 is designed to help resolve this by providing a simple, quick and highly effective format for people to use when journalling. The 3-3-1 journal can be done in just a few minutes, at the end of the day, week or month. The simple format also helps overcome the lack of structure that most people's journalling suffers from, and which itself contributes to procrastination.

The tool is designed to help you review your actions in a positive and structured manner, specifically to counteract negative tendencies that can hinder your objectivity. By focusing on positive language, the tool encourages an objective assessment of your actions, ultimately improving your ability to learn from and improve upon past experiences.

The final question of the three takes a different approach, as it prompts you to consider what you can do to move forward, making it a progressive as well as a review tool. By focusing on a singular action, it allows for more effective change, as concentrated efforts on one thing at a time can yield better results. To get started you'll need nothing more than:

1. A note pad and a pen. Writing accesses a different part of the brain to journalling digitally and is usually more creative. If you prefer a digital journal, there are many available tools you can use.

2. A reminder: something which reminds you to journal regularly. Set yourself a reminder on a diary app or a productivity tool of some sort, or just set your phone alarm on repeat.

3. Five minutes each day or even each week if you prefer. Allow more time for periodic reviews.

And that is it.

The 3-3-1 asks you to reflect at the end of each day, or week, on your actions during that time, and then answer the following questions (do not leave it longer than a week).

3-3-1 IN RELATION TO YOUR TRADING AND RISK PROCESS (DAILY OR WEEKLY)

- What three things did you do well or were you pleased with?
- What three things do you feel you could, or should, have done better?
- What one thing do you feel you should improve upon going forward?

Notes:

Do not write more than one sentence for each point, but keep a space free further down the page below each section to add notes. You may want to add notes about conditions at the time. Or you may want to include an observation on something significant that occurred that week.

MONTHLY AND QUARTERLY 3-3-1

These are not summaries of the 3-3-1s for that month or quarter, but rather fresh entries that look at your trading from a broader perspective. Use the same format as you used for the daily or weekly 3-3-1s.

LOOKING BACK

Try to analyse or review your past 3-3-1s, ideally on a quarterly and an annual basis. Note any repetitive points which keep popping up. If you notice that multiple 3-3-1s include the same one thing you would like to improve going forward, you know where the heavy lifting needs to be done.

PATTERN IDENTIFICATION

When looking back, try to identify behavioural patterns or habitual behaviours. See if there were any which were present during good periods and/or bad periods.

YOUR MIRROR

Think of the 3-3-1s as a mirror. Consider what the words within them reflect about your self.

Are they telling you something about you that you may not have realised? Or are they confirming something about you that you already had a hunch about? Both can be revealing and useful to know.

Is there anything your mirror is revealing that you do not like to see or would prefer to reject? That is what you need to look into. Marcus Aurelius Antoninus, Roman emperor and Stoic philosopher, said, "What stands in the way becomes the way." Whatever it is that you find difficult to accept in your mirror is probably your route forward.

EXAMPLE

During quiet periods in the markets, I would occasionally start looking back over some of my old journals.

In my journals I would write my trade ideas, some thoughts on the markets, and some reflections on what I did. I was not a 'religious' journaler. I would probably write in them every two or three days.

On one occasion I noticed a trade idea I had written down from a couple of years earlier. I was sure the market had followed through successfully on that idea in the subsequent days, but there were no follow-up notes in my journal.

I went into detective mode. I looked back at the price action from the day. Sure enough, it had been a great call. But I looked at my P&L

in my system, and that did not tally with the trade idea I had written down. I went to look at my old trade blotter, where I recorded each trade I transacted, and my scribbled notes.

I noticed that as the market approached my buy level, I had dropped my bid ten ticks. My initial buy level would have been filled, but the new level was not. The market then took off from that level, without me on board. That explained why there were no further notes and the P&L did not seem to tally. "What a dope," I thought.

I wondered if there were any more examples of this. Sure enough, I found a similar situation had occurred a few weeks later. More money left on the table. Then I found another example, and another. This was serial behaviour – some serious behavioural slippage had occurred and I was oblivious to it. The fact that this was a strong trading period made it all the more surprising.

Being aware of this meant I could be more attentive to what I was doing. It also demonstrated the veracity of my calls, which for some reason I was not backing as well as I should.

Another benefit of my looking back was that I noticed patterns of behaviour in my trading that were peculiar to me. These had a very clear and observable track record. If I could harness these in real time, it would be like discovering a favourable card count. These were not chart patterns, they were my own patterns and were to prove very reliable indicators. We all have these, and your journals can help you to identify them.

PART THREE

THE PERFORMANCE PROCESS CYCLE – QUADRANT 2

CHAPTER 16

The Production Phase

Every battle is won or lost before it's ever fought.

Sun Tzu, strategist

THE ACTIVITY ZONES are the transaction 'doing' parts of the Performance Process Cycle, and correspond to two phases. In the first of these phases the trade is produced, while the second covers the performance (where the trade is acted out).

The move into the first of these zones, the Production Phase, commences with a Trigger event. This event makes you aware of a need to explore. It alerts you to a potential opportunity, a threat or something which demands your attention.

The Production Phase is where the trade starts to materialise, though the trader will not yet be physically in the trade. It is the pre-action part of a trade, where a trader forms ideas, theses, or narratives, shapes those ideas into a potential trade, then decides whether to act, and if so how, prior to actual execution.

This is where you bring your full mental capital to bear on the production of the trade. As in the Being Phase, I will explore how people manage to excel in this phase and some of the characteristic aspects which can undermine traders at this point.

THE TRIGGER EVENT

The event that sets a trade into motion is known as the Trigger, and it can come from either an external or internal source. External Triggers include news, data, customer demand, or other external factors that elicit a response. On the other hand, internal Triggers may arise from a trader's feeling, thought, or analysis, research, or sentiment evaluation of the market.

It should be noted that our discussion of the Performance Process Cycle pertains to discretionary trading, which involves human decision-making at some point in the process. This form of trading also encompasses semi-discretionary methods that rely on systemic signals, yet still require the trader to execute or manage the trade manually.

Often the Trigger is a need to manage an existing trade or portfolio. However to keep matters simple, the assumptions I am using refer to the idea of a single trade.

Figure 23 shows the point of transition between the Being and Production phases of the cycle, via a Trigger event.

Figure 23: The Production Phase

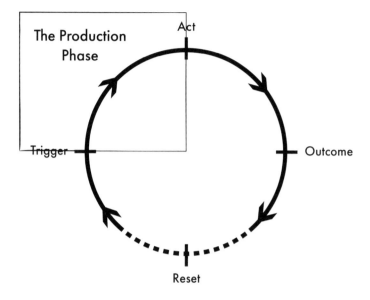

SENSEMAKING AND NARRATIVE FORMATION

The Trigger event takes the trader into a process of 'sensemaking'.

Sensemaking occurs when a trader seeks to make meaning, or sense, of the Trigger and the events around it. As the trader sense-makes, a new or updated narrative is formed in their mind.

Sensemaking may involve a long, detailed process of evaluation, or it can be a very fast process which is highly reactionary and intuitive. Where the trader is using a highly systematic approach, much of this process will be co-opted into the system. The trader's sensemaking process is then simplified – they have to decide whether, when and how to apply a signal.

MOBILISATION

Once a trader's narrative is formed or modified, the trader mobilises to act.

This commences with deciding whether to take the trade or to pass. The Performance Process Cycle is about the trader more than it is about the trade, so even if the trader decides to pass, the cycle remains active until they get mental closure on the idea that the Trigger event initiated. A decision not to act following a Trigger and the process of sensemaking still have consequences which can impact the trader's mental state. In this sense a decision not to trade is still seen as a trade.

The mobilisation process can be as short as a second for intraday traders, or far longer for investment types. The nature of the mobilisation process will vary depending on the trader's approach. However, what is common across all types and approaches is that the trader should act in line with their purpose and process, and should seek to remain present.

In addition to the 3Ps of High Performance discussed in Chapter 9, there are more Ps to consider at this stage: personality, philosophy, planning and preparation. The more aligned a trader is across these Ps, the stronger and more robust their performance is likely to be.

Player-approach traders typically require more thought, planning and preparation in the Production Phase. They are more likely to engage in scenario-planning regarding how to deal with possible courses of action as the market price action unfolds.

House-approach traders work more systematically and reactively. They are more focused on what is happening in the now and deal with the market as it unfolds. Their actions will be largely directed for them by the system or approach they are using and how that requires them to act.

EMOTIONAL PRESSURE
GAUGE HEATS UP

As the Production Phase progresses, the trader's 'emotional pressure gauge' heats up.

During the Being Phase, the trader's degree of emotionality will have been relatively calm, and their ego will have been calmed as they Let Go from the prior cycle. The quietening of the ego, and the turning down of emotionality which resulted, will have enabled their energy levels to rise, which in turn helps to replenish their mental capital.

The grounding, reset and return to calm enable them to ideally return to a calm state of being, which helps them get into an optimal trader state.

However, if a trader does not fully return to an optimal state of being, and thus remains in a sub-optimal trader state, or if they bypass the Reset, their mental capital will be weaker as they enter this vital stage.

When this happens, the potential for poor or sub-par performance increases, and the likelihood of the trader being owned by their ego grows.

Owned traders are prone to acting out of fear (including fear of future regret), falling victim to FOMO and other fear-based actions. They may suffer self-doubt and hesitation. They may seek outside reassurance by asking others what they should do, or they may take the trades of others.

THE PRODUCTION PHASE AND
THE MAY 2007 BUND TRADE

As we saw in Chapter 8, my analysis had identified the potential for a favourable risk-reward setup that could see German government ten-year bond yields rise (and Bund futures move lower). However, I was positioned flat at the time. Two previous attempts at this trade had failed, with losses taken on both trades.

Despite being in the red, I remained in an optimal trader state and was calm as I fully immersed myself in the market.

The Trigger event for this trade was the market's counter-reaction to the release of weak US economic data. Weak data should have seen US yields move lower. However, after a quick adjustment lower in response to the data, yields quickly returned to their previous level.

This return move back to the pre-data-release level was on large volume and steady selling of bonds. Something did not feel right.

I rechecked the details of the US data. It was unambiguously weak; there did not appear to be any room for misinterpretation. However, to be doubly sure I did a quick check-in with our in-house economist, then scanned through the Bloomberg commentary to see the response of other economists and commentators.

There was a clear disconnect between the news and the price action. Since US and German government debt tended to move simultaneously at this time, it would follow that what was happening on US yields would be replicated in German yields.

My narrative was updated by the reaction to this Trigger event. My mind was spinning.

My mobilisation was quick and easy. I had already scenario-planned and prepared a plan of action for how I would transact this trade if the conditions fell into place. I now had to start executing it.

I watched the market intently. I would like to say that at this point I was consciously thinking about what to do, but I was not thinking at all. I was zoned-in, primed to respond.

Around 20 minutes after the release of the US data I started executing the trade with my broker, selling the first chunk of Bunds in my plan and giving them a stop level to watch.

In the Performance Process Cycle, the trader moves from Production to Performance by committing to Act. I will continue describing the execution of this trade when we explore the Performance Phase.

CHAPTER 17

Preparing to Make an Educated Guess

Successful investing is anticipating the anticipations of others.

John Maynard Keynes, economist

J OHN MAYNARD KEYNES's beauty contest analogy remains one of the most apt descriptions of how financial markets work. Keynes compared trading and investing to the beauty contests common at the time in the British newspapers of the 1930s.

In those less politically correct times, the newspapers would print pictures of 100 women. Readers would submit their top six picks of who they thought were the most beautiful. The women whose pictures received the most votes would be the winners, and the readers whose votes were closest to being 'correct' were eligible for a prize.

Keynes stated that to give yourself the best chance to win you should select the face you thought most other people would choose, rather than the one that you thought was the prettiest.

In other words, you should try to gauge what you thought the average opinion was. Then, he added, you should consider that the more sophisticated players would be voting by the same principle. Therefore, to improve your chances further, you should try to infer what the average sophisticated player would be thinking.

Thus, your choice should be based on what you think others think that others will choose. This became known as the Keynesian Beauty Contest theory.

Keynes's purpose behind this concept was to describe how markets work. It also implicitly validates the importance of detached curiosity and seeing things through the lens of others, rather than just through your own lens. This was what Keynes was referring to when he alluded to the need to infer what the average sophisticated player would be thinking. Third level thinking.

MAKING BETTER EDUCATED GUESSES

For all the knowledge, data and information that goes into making a trading or investment decision, the fact remains that each decision is an educated guess.

Your objective as you move into the Production Phase is to manoeuvre into a position from which you can make better educated guesses.

Traders are continually making assessments, based on their observations, analysis and exposure to the opinions of others, while trying to gauge the broader sentiment of the market. They have myriad clues coming their way, many of which are only fleeting.

I used to enjoy playing sudoku on my train journey home from work. Sudoku is a logic-based number puzzle, something like a numerical crossword. The more I played it, the better I got and the faster I could solve the puzzle.

It occurred to me how similar trading is to sudoku. You start with a few clues, try to fathom the answers, eliminate certain options, then try a particular solution. If that does not work, you can eliminate that solution and try a different potential path. You keep doing this until you hit on the only possible answer. As you find more clues, it makes it easier to find subsequent answers.

As you become more skilled at this, your intuitive ability to find logical solutions seems to improve, or maybe it is that you start to trust your intuitive ability more, or maybe it's a combination of both. Whatever is the truth, to use a phrase taken from another type of puzzle, you connect the dots so that you can see the whole picture much more quickly.

To me, trading often felt like a sudoku puzzle, but depending on the time frame you worked in, you only had a very limited time to piece the clues together. The fewer clues you had, and the quicker you could connect the dots to see the bigger picture, the greater the reward. The longer it took to connect the dots, the lower the reward, until it was so marginal that it was not worth taking the risk.

Sometimes, when you are too close, you cannot see the clues. At other times you need to get closer, and sometimes the clues do not mean much to you unless you have vast experience. Other times you can see the clues but don't realise they *are* clues. In the story of the Swiss National Bank from Chapter 7, the head of trading had the benefit of looking from a distance, had vast experience and had the knowledge of where to look for clues.

After observing the clues, and knowing that one of his traders was heavily exposed to an adverse move, he was left with a deeply uncomfortable feeling. He did not know what the SNB would do, but he did not like the situation. He felt that the limited upside of the trade was not worth the risk. If he had waited for his intuitive sense to be confirmed, it would have been too late.

That is making an educated guess. That is risk-taking, risk management, trading.

Traders face several impediments and obstacles which inhibit their ability to effectively make high-quality educated guesses. These include, but are not limited to:

- Holding strong opinions and views that bias their opinion of what they observe. A trader may hold a strong view on a company which makes it difficult to view their results dispassionately.

- Attachments to strong beliefs that prevent them from seeing matters clearly, as Tony did with his bitcoin trade in Chapter 9.

- Their ego being wed to a prevailing narrative which it needs to justify and prove right. Again this happened in Tony's story: he could have exited the trade while he still had a chance to book some profit.

- Seeing the markets as knowable and certain, rather than complex, unknowable and random. Traders who see the world as the latter are more likely to approach it from a perspective of detached curiosity.

- The impact of our natural behavioural biases and our biological limitations. These include loss aversion, our tendency towards confirmation bias, our inability to make good judgements when tired, among many other heuristic biases which sway our ability to exercise true objectivity.

- Our natural tendency to conform to the crowd, led by our ego trying to fulfil its guardianship responsibilities to us. Tony used to loathe the term HODL but became accepting of it in the circles he engaged with.

- Outside pressures, which up the ante on getting positive outcomes. The need to produce an income or return, please stakeholders, and other external life pressures.

- Being on shaky ground. When the situation is insecure, the trader's ego is constantly agitated, this affects their ability to make good-quality choices.

These impediments limit the trader's ability to get into and maintain an optimal trader state, which itself is a prerequisite to accessing a flow state. We explore some of these impediments in more detail in the next couple of chapters.

Working to limit the impact of these impediments will be vital to ensure you are making the most informed decisions you can.

Some traders go to extraordinary lengths to get themselves and their mindset prepared for the battle they face. One trader I coached, who exemplifies this is Amrit Sall. The following excerpt is from Jack Schwager's interview with Amrit from *Unknown Market Wizards*:

> Before a significant trade event, I go through breath work and meditation to centre in on my present moment and transcend the chatter in my mind. Over time, I have learned how to access flow states within a few minutes. The ability to access flow is fundamental for success in trading and many other endeavours, such as professional sports. When I am deeply present, everything feels easy. In this 'deep now' state, I'm reacting from a subconscious level that represents 95% of the mind's potential versus 5% for the conscious mind. In this state, I'm creative, and I can process large amounts of information and react without hesitation. I'm open to new information and evolve my positions accordingly. Trading feels easy, and I'm not trying to force anything, I have no attachment to my position or the outcome. I cut losses without hesitation, and I run my winners without any impulse to snatch profits.

Amrit was and remains an exceptional trader. His approach is focused on being primed for the moment.

Another excellent trader I worked with, who is an award-winning fund manager, focuses on setting his environment to be optimal. He deliberately made a point of locating himself outside of the major financial centres. Removing himself from the bubbles and echo chambers which enabled him to view the markets with distance and objectivity. This helped him to have a more balanced and nuanced perspective that was not influenced by local market myopia.

In the book *Sensemaking* (Hachette, 2017), Christian Madsbjerg tells of how Robert Johnson, Soros Fund's chief currency specialist, went to live in Helsinki for a few months in the winter of 1991.

Johnson had huge exposure to the Finnish currency, and his temporary relocation and physical immersion were to provide him with great insights that were not contained in any data. Johnson was a player-approach trader extraordinaire. He had a view, but he also wanted to be in the terrain.

As a trader you are entering the unknown every moment of every day, and from there you need to make well-informed educated guesses. Mastering the mental game requires you to be primed to act optimally in that moment.

CHAPTER 18

The Map Is Not the Terrain

No man ever steps in the same river twice. For it's not the same river and he's not the same man.

Heraclitus, philosopher

Take a look at Figure 24. What do you see?

Figure 24

The answer you give will, to a large degree, depend on how the question is framed. In my initial question, there was no framing. But if I were to ask you, "Can you see two white heads facing each other?" you would probably see those white heads. If I asked, "Can you see a black classical vase with a wide base and a wide brim?" you would probably see that.

Context is everything.

This is also the case with trading and investing. Traders make decisions in a torrent of information, data, insight and opinions which bias their perspectives. Context is everything, and so it is vital to have the right 'map'.

Every trade you take is based on information and data that helps you make an educated guess. However, no matter how well informed you feel you are, there is always going to be some data or information that is unknown and unknowable.

Figure 25 is a reproduction of a screenshot taken from my phone on the afternoon of the Brexit referendum. This was a nationwide referendum held in the UK on 23 June 2016 that asked people to vote on whether the UK should remain in the European Union (EU).

The screenshot showed the betting odds on a British betting exchange, which mediates bids and offers on various betting outcomes.

Figure 25: Brexit referendum betting odds

Betting Slip		
Time 14:56 Date 23rd June 2016		
EU UK Membership Referendum		
In-Play	**Back**	**Lay**
In favour of staying in the EU	1.23	1.24
In favour of leaving the EU	5.3	5.4

The betting odds implied that the probability of the UK voting to leave the EU was just 19%.

Yet within a few hours of the vote closing, it was clear the UK populace had voted to leave.

RIGHTNESS

It is in this complex and unknowable world that traders must make educated guesses. They are not helped by the ego's need to be right, nor by our various education systems and social structures, in which being right – 'rightness' – is the golden ticket for advancement.

As a schoolchild you were praised and rewarded for being right. This continued as you went through school, college, and then into the world of work.

Our education prepares us for a deterministic world; a world where everything can be explained, predicted, and understood. This is the map the first 20-plus years of our life instils us with. This is the wrong map for a world where you have to live by making educated guesses.

The map of the world that most of us carry says that the world is knowable, understandable, explainable. This map sees the world as complicated, but as a place where everything can be understood through reductive processes. This reduces problems to recipes and formulas.

The real world is complex, not complicated. A complex world cannot be controlled and predicted; problems cannot be simply explained by reducing them to their most basic form.

In this complex world, solutions derived from a complicated world map fall short.

Not everyone holds this complicated map of the world. When you realise that the world will not bend to your will, you see things differently.

An anecdotal observation, shared between me and some coaching colleagues, is that there is a high prevalence of successful traders who suffered some sort of early life trauma.

We suspect that their life experiences endowed them with the complex mental map of the world. Life demonstrates to these people, at an early age, that the world will not conform to their wishes but will instead take them on a path of its own choosing.

These traumas may have been devastating one-off events or ongoing traumas suffered throughout their early lives and school years.

Another group who seem significantly overrepresented amongst successful traders are dyslexics. There could be any number of reasons for this, but some interesting data suggests that they found their journey through their education system was traumatic.

In a study researching adult dyslexics, conducted in the UK, all participants stated that they had experienced emotional trauma during their time in education. Yet a study of self-made millionaires in the UK found that 40% were dyslexic, a pretty staggering figure when it is estimated only about 10% of people are dyslexic.[3]

In the US, research found that barely 2% of dyslexics who enrolled in undergraduate programmes completed the requisite four years of study.[4] And yet, former Cisco CEO John Chambers (himself a dyslexic) estimates that 25% of CEOs are dyslexic – although he says that most do not want to talk about it.[5]

I realise that I am making unscientific leaps here to try to prove a point, but it is not just people dealing with trauma and dyslexics who seem to be overrepresented among the highly successful traders I meet. I have come across a significant number of people with learning difficulties such as ADHD, autism, bipolar disorder, borderline personality disorders and dyspraxia. I would speculate that most of these, as a result of their early life traumas, also carry the complex world map.

By contrast I have noticed that many people from highly academic backgrounds are challenged when it comes to taking and running risk. They often carry a map which sees the world as complicated. Their view of the world is seen through a lens that says there is an answer, we just need to figure it out, and we will achieve rightness.

This was the trap which the 'geniuses' at Long-Term Capital management (LTCM) fell into before the fund failed, as did 'the smartest guys in the room' at Enron before its collapse. More recently, it appears to be the trap which the whiz-kids at FTX have fallen into.

There are some notable exceptions to this, such as mathematicians and engineers, whose disciplines provide a grounding for a complex-world perspective. Perhaps it is not surprising that the world's most successful hedge fund was started by a mathematician, Jim Simons, and consists almost entirely of mathematicians and engineers.

My point here is not anti-academic, far from it, it is just sharing some observations myself and others have noticed.

In a complicated world, outlier events are considered so unlikely as to be unworthy of consideration. In a complex world, black, white and grey swan events are given consideration and are viewed as being much more likely than other people realise.

Being conscious of the possibility of such events is the correct map to have. George Soros, himself someone who grew up in very traumatic circumstances, identified a potential grey swan when he predicted that the UK would drop out of the ERM in 1992.

(A grey swan is an event that is known and possible to happen, but which is assumed to be unlikely to occur. The term derives from Naseem Taleb's Black Swan theory.)

CONDITIONS ON
THE GROUND

During the UK's Covid-19 lockdowns, like many people, I found myself going on walks in the area where I lived. Despite having been a resident of that area for almost three decades, I had barely taken the time to walk the surrounding streets. Walking in my area enabled me to find out so much more about it.

Even when we have the right map, this does not mean we know the terrain. A map does not tell us what conditions are like on the ground. Similarly, navigating the markets requires you to get down and dirty.

Jim Simons, founder of the hedge fund Renaissance Technologies, did not hit the ground running despite his eventual fantastic success. He first spent over a decade feeling his way through the terrain. Later it was his understanding of the terrain that led to him dialling down the algorithms at his fund for a time in 2007, when algorithmic trading firms were hit by what was known as the 'quant quake'.

Despite using a system that would be defined as a solution on a complicated map, Simons ultimately worked from the complex map, where he knew the terrain. He knew not to commit unlimited capital despite appearing to have the solution, which was why he capped the size of the fund.

I have read many people accuse Simons of making an error with this decision, those people are theorists, not realists. Simons was both. Unlike the theorists at LTCM, who did not have any sense of the conditions on the ground.

[LTCM was a hedge fund founded in 1994 by a group of finance professionals, including Nobel Prize-winning economists. The fund, a house-approach trading business, used complex trading strategies and high leverage to generate large returns for its investors. However, in 1998, the fund experienced significant losses due to the Russian financial crisis leading to the collapse of the hedge fund with losses estimated to be around $4bn.]

Likewise, George Soros's Bank of England trade in Chapter 5 was not based on data and knowledge alone. Soros studied the terrain too. He made a point of attending press conferences held by Helmut Schlesinger, the head of Germany's Bundesbank.

At one press conference, Soros had a chance to put a question to Schlesinger. He asked whether he agreed with the goal of a European Currency. Schlesinger replied that he liked the idea but that he was only interested in one name for that currency: the Deutschmark.

From that moment, for Soros and his team, the die was cast on their Bank of England trade.

It is easy to carry the wrong map, and even when you have the right map it can be a mistake to rely on the map alone. The map the captain of the *Titanic* had did not tell him about the icebergs in the terrain of the North Atlantic. The world is far more complex than the maps we carry. The geniuses of LTCM, Enron and FTX all assumed that their maps were sufficient.

Systems, processes, frameworks, models: they all try to simplify complexity, but they don't eliminate it. They never can.

CHAPTER 19

Our Natural Limitations

We're blind to our blindness. We have very little idea of how little we know. We're not designed to know how little we know.

Daniel Kahneman, Nobel Prize-winning psychologist

HAVE YOU EVER formed a queue without realising you were forming a queue?

After the first covid lockdown, I travelled into Central London with my wife to meet our daughter. As we walked around near where she lived, we came to a small grocery store. My wife and daughter went inside to look for a few items, while I waited outside.

During the lockdown it had become customary to queue to get into larger stores. And though queueing comes easy to us Brits, this grocery store was not a busy shop, and there was no queueing system required to enter.

While waiting I leaned up against the front of the store and started looking at the internet on my phone. I was probably lost in reading about my favourite football team, the mighty Arsenal. After about ten minutes my wife and daughter emerged from the store, and we continued down the street. As we walked away, I heard a disapproving "tut-tut" from someone behind me. I looked back and noticed a queue of about 20 disgruntled people had formed behind me as I stood there looking at my phone. There had been no one else in the store, so there had been no need to queue.

This is an example of something very natural to us humans, and not just us Brits: our need to conform.

The need to conform has become a staple of prank TV shows. The original prank show was a series from the 1960s called *Candid Camera*. One of its most famous episodes, from 1962, was called 'Face the Rear'. If you google 'Face The Rear', you can watch a clip from this episode.

The prank was played on a person who had entered an empty elevator. They stood facing the doors, as you would expect. Three of the *Candid Camera* crew then entered, seemingly independently. Each one faced towards the rear of the elevator, instead of the doors. The cameras then zoomed in on the person being pranked. They now seemed unsure of themselves and started showing signs of awkwardness. Slowly they started turning towards the rear of the elevator, even though that was clearly the wrong way. Eventually they were fully facing the rear of the elevator.

If we go back to thinking of the ego in dialogue with its 'host', I imagine this person's ego was shouting to them, "Turn around, everyone is facing the back! You look stupid!" The host may have initially pushed back against their ego, saying meekly, "But the door is at the front." But the ego then fires back, "You just look ridiculous, do what everyone else is doing!"

The show repeated a number of famous experiments carried out by noted Gestalt psychologist Soloman Asch, which demonstrated the influence of group pressure on people.

This same influence is at work in markets. Markets are a crowd, and they impact us individually.

It is not just our ego's need to be right, or the carrying of the wrong map, or our need to conform that is problematic. We work and function in many ways which seemingly impact our ability to act rationally.

Like the ego, these behaviours are possibly rooted in our mammalian ancestry, and have a survival element to them.

The paradigm put forward in the behavioural finance world is that these behaviours are irrational. In a complicated reductionist world, one could see that argument. But in the real world, the context is different.

Firstly, the real world is complex, and secondly, our understanding of our self is different. We are not thinkers whose thoughts get corrupted by our feelings, we are feelers whose feelings inform our thoughts and contribute to our mental capital, as the head of trading in the SNB example did. This is not just my view, it is one that is increasingly being verified by studies in neuroscience. Harvard Business School professor Gerald Zaltman believes that 95% of all cognition occurs in the subconscious mind.[6]

When framed through the lens of evolution and the need to survive, it may be that our natural behavioural tendencies, which are often judged as irrational, are perfectly rational. There is nothing more rational than wanting to survive.

If we want to have a better relationship with our self, understanding these elements can be helpful. If we find we are following the herd, we should remember that we are not flawed but actually quite normal. It can also help us understand why the markets do what they do. They are a thundering herd; that is, until they are attacked by a group of bears and disperse.

Understanding our natural biases can also be helpful. Cognitive biases are generally defined as being systematic errors in reasoning. This definition works if you assume we are programmed robots working in a complicated rather than a complex landscape. But we are not, and the landscape is not a laboratory. So, our biases are not bugs or flaws, they are simply how we are wired.

The list of cognitive biases has grown exhaustive in the past few years. The following section covers just a small selection of the many out there. Like all people, traders are prone to acting on these biases, and their influence is likely to be more pronounced when we are in a sub-optimal trader state.

LOSS AVERSION

Loss aversion is a bias which states that we mentally feel the pain of a loss roughly twice as much as we feel the joy from an equal gain.

The early work on this concept was conducted by psychologists Daniel Kahneman and the late Amos Tversky. We see the subtle influence of loss aversion in many of the classic behavioural errors of traders and investors.

It is loss aversion which causes traders to grab at profits, since they are so fearful of them disappearing. Yet at the same time they run losses, because they so want to avoid the pain which comes from crystallising a loss.

The term 'sell your losers and run your winners' is generally used by traders to counter this loss aversion tendency. I would however add that this needs a context. It works for player-approach traders, whereas house-approach traders might actually benefit from working the other way around. Context matters.

Loss aversion is a natural behaviour. Experiments on capuchin monkeys have demonstrated how our primate relatives also suffer from this bias.

Our natural loss aversion tends to pervade everything we do. Even our tendency to not want to look inward at ourselves could be a factor of loss aversion. We may fear the negative consequences of what we find more than twice as much as we are drawn to the potential benefits.

I do wonder whether there was loss aversion at work when I met the traders at the Hong Kong hedge fund in Chapter 13. It is possible that they feared the loss of face from seeking help more than twice as powerfully as they considered the potential benefits they would get from coaching.

CONFIRMATION BIAS

As a trader I was highly prone to confirmation bias. This is a tendency to seek information that supports our pre-existing beliefs and ignores contradictory information.

During one challenging period, relatively early in my career when I was a proprietary trader at Credit Suisse, I was in a deeply sub-optimal state. I started seeking articles that corroborated my positions and my views on the market. If an article was neutral, I would mine it to find the argument that agreed with me. I avoided articles which I could see held an opposing view to mine. I also veered towards talking with the traders who shared my view.

This is the opposite of what I did later in my career, when I would try to deconstruct my trading ideas, much like you try to disprove the validity of a number in a sudoku puzzle in order to find the correct number. If my idea still stood up, that meant I had a strong argument, just like when Soros heard Schlesinger's reply and knew his idea was even stronger. When the bond and bund futures could not sustain a rally on very weak economic data, that was a strong clue that my Bund trade might be in play.

Confirmation bias can be deadly. Tony, from the bitcoin story in Chapter 9, told me how he took solace from speaking with those who shared his views when things turned against him. At the same time, traders who exited their long positions were seen by them as traitors. When the bears attack, the bulls turn on each other.

THE ENDOWMENT EFFECT

The endowment effect is a another bias common in trading. It happens when a person places a higher value on an object they already own than they would on that same object if they did not own it. The object does not have to be a physical object, it can be a belief or a point of view.

Essentia Analytics is a company which provides behavioural analytics and performance consulting services for asset managers. In 2022 they produced a report which documented 10,000 investments across 43 separate portfolios over 14 years. They identified a strong pattern of investors holding on to positions too long, which led to diminishing returns over the lifecycle of the investments.[7]

Their report noted that "behavioural biases are highly relevant when trying to understand the drivers of trends in alpha." They suspected that the endowment effect is a significant factor which contributes to investors holding on to positions too long, contributing to sub-par performance. Once the asset managers owned the stocks, their ability to hold an objective view of them became compromised.

THE WARPED RUDDER

A useful analogy for the impact of these biases and our behavioural limitations is to liken them to being a slightly warped rudder on a boat you are trying to steer. You point the boat in the direction you want it to go, then assume you are heading in the right direction, but the slight warp in the rudder shifts you off course.

We do not see the warped rudder. It is below the waterline, and the warp is so mild as to not even be obvious to the human eye, but it is always there. We have to learn to steer our boat in the right direction despite the warped rudder, using navigational aids. But the effort of doing this slowly and subtly tires us. We can only keep going for so long before our ability to keep adjusting becomes compromised, and we go off in the wrong direction.

CHAPTER 20

Mental Capital, Time of Day and Decision-Making

I do my high-IQ meetings before lunch. Like, anything that's going to be really mentally challenging, that's a 10 o'clock meeting. By 5pm, I'm like, 'I can't think about that today. Let's try this again tomorrow at 10am.'

Jeff Bezos, founder of Amazon

ALI HAD WORKED on a bank FX trading desk for 15 years when the bank announced it was moving to algorithmic trading. In 2013 he, along with most of the bank's FX traders, was made redundant. While Ali was searching for a new job, he started trading for himself. He had no plans to make this permanent, he merely wanted to keep his hand in while searching for a new role.

At first Ali did not enjoy trading from home, his preference was to work on another bank trading desk with other traders as part of a franchise book, as he had always done. But as time passed, and his job search was proving fruitless, he started to make some decent money for himself from his FX day-trading activities.

He began to acclimatise to working from home, and eventually committed to trading for himself. He gave himself three years to see if he could make it work. It was a very different challenge. He had no flow, and no client centricity or information edge, but he always had a good read on the market.

By the time we were introduced, Ali had been trading for himself for around five years. In the previous two years he had made between £3m and £4m each year – far more than he had been paid at the bank. By now he had a small office in London, with an assistant/analyst.

His was a rare tale of someone leaving a sell-side trading role and making a successful adjustment to trading their own money.

Ali told me how he worked and functioned. He was not unlike Amrit Sall in some ways, getting himself mentally primed for trading each day.

What I found most remarkable about Ali was that he would stop trading at 1pm. He would not take any more trades after that, even if he felt there was a good opportunity.

He spent his afternoons assessing the morning's work, reviewing past performance, updating his longer-term market views and prepping for the next day.

I was fascinated by this working style. I asked him what lay behind his decision to work this way.

He told me how, during analysis of his work, he had noticed he was more controlled and profitable in the mornings and less so in the afternoons. He decided to start conducting some deeper analysis of his performance, based on time of day. He drew a chart on a piece of paper which looked roughly like Figure 26. It showed his typical performance by the hour.

Figure 26: Ali's performance over the course of a day

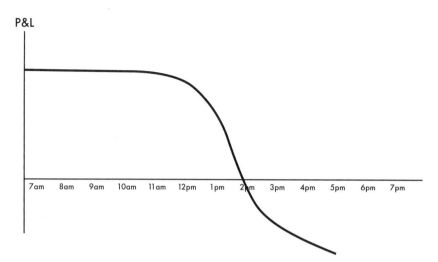

Ali made money most mornings, but lost money most afternoons. The same pattern played out almost every day, and until his analysis he had been totally oblivious to it.

He calculated that if he was making on average £5,000 a day, that would increase to an average of £7,500 a day if he just stopped trading in the afternoon.

He said, "It was like every lunchtime going to the bank, drawing out a wad of £2,500 in bank notes, coming back, throwing the wad in a bin, pouring petrol on it, then tossing in a lighted match. Every single day."

At first he tried to get better at afternoon trading, but he just was not able to do it. Eventually, he decided to commit more to the morning trading. So, he forced himself not to trade in the afternoon. He said it was not easy at first, he was itching to get involved in the afternoons, but as he started seeing the results in his improved performance he became better at resisting the urge.

After seeing tangible results in his aggregate P&L, he felt more confident to increase his size, which he did gradually until he was doing double his previous size.

As a pure house-approach trader, he worked on a standard position size, rather than strategic position sizing.

PAROLE BOARD JUDGES

A few years prior to working with Ali, I came across some fascinating research reported in a *New York Times* article under the headline, 'Do You Suffer From Decision Fatigue?'[8]

The story told of research carried out by a group of psychologists in Israel, who had assessed the decision-making practices of a group of parole board judges.

The judges had a binary decision to make: either grant parole, or deny it.

Each prisoner up for parole had earned the right to be reviewed by a parole board. The case was then sent to the judges, who made an assessment, interviewed the prisoner and then decided whether to grant or deny parole.

The researchers found that at the beginning of the day, a judge was likely to give a favourable ruling to grant parole about 65% of the time. However, as the day wore on, the generosity of the judge's decisions diminished. By late afternoon, the possibility of a prisoner getting a favourable decision was no better than about 10%. There were very short-lived improvements after breaks in which the judges had been able to take some nourishment.

What appeared to be happening was that the more decisions the judges made throughout the day, and the more brainpower they exerted, the lower the quality of their decisions became. Their mental capital was depleting.

First thing in the morning, the judges were able to think clearly and would rationally weigh up all the pros and cons of why the prisoner should be granted parole. By the late afternoon, they would fall back on biases and lazy thinking.

TIME OF DAY DECISION-MAKING

A lesser-known piece of research analysed the decision-making behaviours of users of the Free Internet Chess Server (FICS) to assess the time of day that players made their best decisions. The study found that the most accurate decisions were made between 8am and 1pm.[9]

I also came across a piece of private research on the website DailyFX. com which analysed the decisions of thousands of FX day trading clients of a brokerage firm over the period of one year to show profitability by hour of day. Figure 27 is a replication of the chart in EURUSD.

Since the majority of FX trading is done in Europe, with the UK alone accounting for 43% of FX trading globally in 2019 compared to only 16% in the US, the chart has been redrawn to show only European trading hours.

Figure 27: Percentages of trades in EURUSD closed with a profit, by the hour for retail FX traders over the course of one year

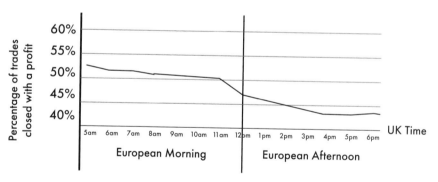

Source: Traits of Successful Traders, DailyFX.com -
https://www.dailyfx.com/forex/technical/article/special_report/2013/01/24/forex_education_do_hours_i_trade_matter.html

Percentage of trades in EURUSD closed with a profit. The data is derived from Forex Capital Markets LLC accounts. (Excluding Managed and Eligible Contract Participant accounts). Data taken from 10/01/2009 to 09/30/2010 rounded to the nearest whole number.

The image is a redrawing of the EURUSD data only, for just the European trading session.

OUR ABSENT MENTAL CAPITAL GAUGE

Our mental capital, which powers the decisions we make in our trading, is subject to the realities of our human biology. Mental capital can be thought of like a muscle. The more it gets used, the more tired it gets and the less effectively it functions.

This is what happens when we try to steer the boat constantly with the warped rudder. Bit by bit, this tires us. Eventually, we cannot steer any more; we cannot fight the warped rudder. While Ali discovered this in his case, it is not something we are usually aware of. He adjusted his process by reducing the amount of time he devoted to steering. He turned the boat off at 1pm every day and dropped anchor.

It would be wonderful if we could have a gauge which could tell us when our lack of mental capital is becoming problematic. Unfortunately, we do not have one, so we keep on acting as if we can think clearly.

Many parts of our biological system have indicators which help us assess when we need to pull back. If we lift weights, our muscles get tired, and we pull back from exercising those muscles. When we are hungry or thirsty, we know we need to find food or water. We get tired and know we need sleep. But we do not get bio-feedback about our thinking capacity.

In the absence of this mental capacity gauge, the traders may want to consider exploring the structure of their day and working hours, so that they can operate at their best. Longer-term, less-active traders can go longer, but their thinking will still be compromised as the day progresses. They may want to avoid big decisions later in the day. Sleeping on such decisions would be a sound option.

Fast, highly active traders may want to add some structure to their day if they wish to trade into the afternoon. Perhaps build in breaks and plan shorter stints. Age may also prove to be a factor in how long people can remain mentally effective.

It could be a valuable exercise to make long-term assessments of when you are at your best. We all have different circadian rhythms.

Our mental capital is a precious and finite resource. It has to be managed carefully.

Many high-profile decision-makers are known to engage in actions which reduce the number of decisions they have to make. Mark Zuckerberg wears the same T-shirt every day. During his presidency, Barack Obama would only have a small number of suits to choose from, so that he could focus his mental energy on the major decisions he had to make. Jeff Bezos, as the quote at the start of this chapter highlights, holds his 'high-IQ meetings' before lunch.

CHAPTER 21

Intuition and Trading

We are not thinking machines that feel, rather we are feeling machines that think.

Antonio Damasio, neuroscientist

THE FIREFIGHTER

THE PSYCHOLOGIST GARY Klein is one of the world's leading experts on decision-making under conditions of uncertainty. He spent many years interviewing people whose jobs required them to make split-second life-or-death decisions.

During one interview, the commander of a firefighting crew told Klein about an incident in which he made a 'decision' that he felt was down to divine intervention.

His crew had been fighting what seemed to be a standard house fire when, on a split-second call, he ordered everyone to leave the building. As the last firefighter left the house, the floor they had been standing on collapsed. Any firefighter standing there would have plunged into an inescapable furnace.

This account triggered something in Klein that caused him to delve deeper.

Klein asked probing questions of the commander's recollection of the events of this incident. As he did so, the commander explained how he felt that certain things did not add up. There was a disconnect between what he usually experienced and the situation on that occasion.

He recalled that the fire felt 'too quiet' and yet, at the same time, his ears felt hotter than they should in that situation. The combination of these sensations prompted a reaction in him. He did not have time to piece the clues together into a coherent explanation of events or a set of choices; he just knew something was not right, and ordered his crew out.

It transpired that the epicentre of the fire was not on the first floor, where the firefighters were standing, but, unusually for this type of house, in a basement that they had not realised existed.

The decision made in that moment may have indeed felt like divine intervention, but Klein's questioning made it clear that the commander's intuition had informed him that something was not right, and his experience told him that he needed to order everyone out.

This particular moment was a significant turning point in Klein's research as it suggested that individuals tend to rely on their intuition, also known as tacit knowledge, especially in high-pressure situations that are uncertain and fast-paced. Experienced individuals have the advantage of relying on familiar patterns of behaviour to aid them in making decisions.

This ability is what great traders – and great performers in all fields – do, as several stories through this book have suggested, and which this next story emphasises.

THE FX ARBITRAGER

In the highly liquid FX markets, market-making traders' ability to generate spread income is negligible due to the tight bid-offer spread of the traded prices. To produce additional income, FX traders need to develop highly skilled trading capabilities with which they can apply their tacit knowledge (intuition) to their work.

One trader I was working with had developed and honed his abilities at a bank over more than a decade. When I asked this trader how he adds value, he replied that he arbitrages FX. I looked at him, bewildered.

I did not believe that anyone was able to truly arbitrage FX in the major high-liquid currencies. Since the 1980s, computerised trading had made it near impossible for a trader to be able to do this. However, he insisted that arbitrage was what he did. I was not going to argue with him; he made a lot of money, so he was obviously doing something very right.

I was, however, curious. So I explored this further, probing in an attempt to unpick the nuance behind his method. What I discerned was that he used very rapid, intuitive trading, based on observation, sensing and highly developed pattern-recognition skills.

Having done this over many years, he had honed his technique. He had become highly synchronised with the microscopic fluctuations of price, and synthesised the intense flow of news, insights and information which would only be noise to anyone else.

His technique only worked when he applied it to the triangulation of currency pairs, which traders used to do when they arbitraged spot FX. This understandably made him feel as if he too was arbitraging FX.

For this house-approach trader, his production process was very short and largely systematic. He did not have to think about production, he just played out the system which he had created and then trusted his self to execute it.

When this system went wrong, it was usually because his ego had become agitated. This would happen if he went off-process or took trades outside his highly systematised approach.

It would also go wrong if his rhythm was upset, or he was thrown off balance by an external disturbance, a difficult colleague, a manager's comment or a client matter. This would trigger his ego, which then tried to take control of this trading.

INTUITION IS THE GIFT

If I had a pound for every time I had read, "Don't listen to your gut when trading", I probably would never have had to worry about making money from trading ever.

In Chapter 16's description of the May 2007 Bund trade, I used the phrase, "There was a clear disconnect between the news and the price action." That sentence may seem like it was based on a rational assessment of what was happening, but it was not. I only noticed the disconnect because my senses picked up on it. Something felt off. My experience and senses were telling me that this was an unusual pattern of behaviour. If I had waited to make a rational conclusion of what was happening before concluding that this was a signal I should heed, it would have been far too late to act, the market would have moved and the opportunity would have been missed.

In the world of trading and investing, intuition often gets a bad rap. Many believe that the only force behind the decisions made by traders and investors is intellectual brainpower applied to economic theories, and that unless we have a grasp on these, we should not act. However, this mindset undermines the importance and value of intuition in the decision-making process.

Emotions and intuition are often seen as messy and counterproductive. In his book *Minding the Markets* (Palgrave Macmillan, 2011), Professor

David Tuckett interviewed 50 leading fund managers to get a sense of what really happens in the emotionally charged world of financial trading. One excerpt from the book which leapt out at me stated:

> While emotion may create states of mind that lead to error, using it and intuition may be either the only or the best way to produce effective, fast, and adapted decision-making, an argument increasingly supported by cognitive neuroscience.

DEMYSTIFYING INTUITION

The mechanics behind intuition are not well understood. However, there is a developing body of understanding and competing theories which has emerged, inspired by advances in neuroscience, over the past few decades.

The vital role of intuition and emotions in even basic decision-making is now accepted within the scientific community, thanks in large part to the work of a team of behavioural scientists at the University of Iowa.

In 1994 this team, consisting of Antoine Bechara, Antonio Damasio, Hanna Damasio and Steven Anderson, devised a card game which aimed to simulate real-life decision making.[10]

The game required players to pick cards from one of four card decks (named A, B, C and D). The participant could win or lose money with each card. The game was rigged so that when a player picked a card, they would earn either a large or a small reward depending on which card was chosen. As the players turned over cards, they would get information which could help them identify how the game was rigged.

To help the researchers, players were hooked up to a device similar to a lie detector, which measured their skin conductance response to identify minor changes in their stress levels.

As the game was played, the researchers asked the players to observe when they felt they knew the pattern which was most optimal for winning.

Most players developed a strong feeling – a hunch – about the pattern after turning about 50 cards, though it was not until they had turned 80 cards that most could recognise the pattern with enough certainty that they could clearly state it.

However, changes in their skin conductivity, which suggested they may be picking up on the pattern, were already being registered once they had turned over just ten cards.

This is how we work. We *kind of* know, well before we *do* know, and often even before we think we might know.

But we don't trust 'kind of'– perhaps wisely sometimes. Despite this, if we wait until we know for sure, that is often too late. Great traders learn to trust their instincts, then develop the ability to integrate them into a structured process to achieve optimal results.

The FX trader in this story did this, and this was his edge. George Soros did this, according to his son Robert, who said his father adjusts his market positions when he feels physical discomfort in his back. "It has nothing to do with reason. He literally goes into spasm, and it's this early warning sign."

It is something that even the maths geniuses at Jim Simon's Renaissance Technologies did. Robert Mercer, one of the senior portfolio managers at Renaissance, said "The signals that we have been trading without interruption for fifteen years make no sense." Mercer was saying that they go with their intuition on signals, and work from there.

In the story of the firefighter at the beginning of this chapter, the commander's intuitive abilities saved the lives of his entire crew. He did not have time to think about why he was feeling the way he was, or what the logic behind it was. He just acted.

This happens in trading too. As you become more experienced, you pick up signals felt internally. But, if you wait to confirm the logic, often it can be too late to take the opportunities or deal with threats.

Intuition allows us to connect the dots much quicker. It allows us to read the signs and signals coming from our probing actions in the markets. This allows our map to be updated to include new and changing features of the terrain.

As Antonio Damasio says, "We are not thinking machines that feel, rather we are feeling machines that think."

CHAPTER 22

Learning to Trust Your Intuition

The intuitive mind is a sacred gift and the rational mind is a faithful servant. We have created a society that honours the servant and has forgotten the gift.

Albert Einstein, physicist

LEARNING TO DEVELOP your intuition is an inner-game skill. However, the ego and our distrust of intuition can play a mendacious role in stifling its development and holding back our performance more generally.

Failure to develop intuitive skills is a hidden tax on the trader's bottom line. It contributes to behavioural slippage and thus mediocrity. One trader who would not accept his mediocrity was Graham.

Graham worked for a US hedge fund. He described his performance during his first three years there as, "Okay, but not setting the world on fire." His annual returns averaged around 4%. This was just about acceptable in a low-interest environment and given his very low P&L volatility, but he felt he could do better.

Graham ran a fixed income relative value portfolio, the bond market equivalent of a long-short equity strategy. He was able to take directional risk to add value to the portfolio, but he was struggling in this regard.

Whenever I work with a new client, I ask them to complete two psychometric profiles and a reflective trading questionnaire. Graham's response to one question – what he would like to address in the performance coaching – was revealing.

> I would like to understand and correct what is hindering me from expressing many of the trades that I wish to do, most notably in the macro directional space but across the board. There is a clear disconnect between the guttural or fundamental views that I have on a regular basis and the amount of risk (if any at all) that I'm willing to take on the view. I would like to correct this. In essence, I want to learn how to trust my own sense of judgement and conviction.

His response when asked to identify his three trading demons highlighted how this issue manifested.

1. Cutting positions early due to losses.

2. Doing recommended trades from the street.

3. Taking profits far too early.

There were many more 'trading demons' which he came to reveal, including: impatience, fear of missing out, hesitation leading to not taking trades, poor sizing and high levels of self-doubt.

As always, these were symptoms of deeper issues rather than the issues themselves.

Also of crucial importance was how he answered the risk philosophy question in his reflective questionnaire. This is the question I posed at the start of Chapter 7.

Which of these do you resonate with the most?

You never go broke taking a profit.

You never go broke taking a loss.

Graham responded with 'You never go broke taking a loss'. This suggested that Graham had a player-approach philosophy, even though as a Relative Value trader he was using a house-approach style.

Psychometrics can reveal powerful insights about a trader. They are particularly useful when they hint at some sort of divergence between what might be expected of a trader and what they are implying. One of the psychometrics hinted at a divergence in alignment between *who* Graham was and *how* he was, as a risk-taker.

The Risk Type Compass is a psychometric that identifies people as being characterised by one of eight different risk types. Anecdotally, I have noticed a high degree of correlation between a trader's risk type and the styles and methods they employ.

Most RV (Relative Value) traders tend to work in very structured and deliberate ways, deploying large amounts of risk and managing it in a systematic portfolio style. This style of working is well aligned to the risk types that are deliberate and evidence-based, and less inclined to make decisions on the fly.

By contrast, Graham's risk type has a preference for intuition-based decision-making. Traders who work in this way tend to place directional risk, often surfing on the back of market momentum then exiting trades as the momentum wanes.

THE SELF-IMAGE

I probed away, asking Graham questions and trying to understand these apparent paradoxes.

But Graham's self-image was getting in the way. If you recall, our self-image is carefully crafted and honed by us, in collusion with our ego. It typically conforms to the type of person our ego would like us to be seen as.

The self-image reflexively resists being challenged, lest it crumble.

When our self-image is close to our true, or core, self, it is easier to be present and to bring the full power of our self to what we do. However, the less aligned our core self is with our self-image, the more challenging it becomes for us to be authentic and bring the true power of our self to the tasks we face.

No one is immune to this. It is rare that our self-image is an exact overlay of our true self.

In the world of investment banks and hedge funds, people tend to build a self-image that fits in with the culture of the world they work in. Thus, it tends to emphasise someone successful, who uses logical thinking processes and evidence-based approaches.

Though Graham, ironically, was closely aligned to his true self, even then there was a conflict between his true self and his self-image.

This had been implied by the divergence between his responses to the questionnaires and psychometrics and was apparent in his embarrassment when talking about his intuitive abilities.

Graham shared that he had many, mostly inspired, short-term directional trading ideas, in both the rates and FX spaces. But he had trouble getting behind these trades.

At one point he giggled like a naughty child, then told me how he had recently made some good money trading in and out of the FX market.

Much like the commander's intuition in the firefighter story, these trades felt like divine inspiration. But divine inspiration did not fit with the narrative of Graham's self-image.

As a result, Graham frequently found himself avoiding trades, entering in small size, or lacking the confidence to stick with his trades. He would then watch helplessly as the trades moved significantly in his favour, leading to deep frustration and anger.

Sometimes, when we explored these issues, Graham would throw up excuses for himself. Excuses are an ego-defence mechanism, a form of deflection.

This felt like self-sabotage. Graham's strong intuitive senses were leading him to outstanding trade ideas, but taking these trades was a threat to his self-image. He had succumbed to a sense he should be, or act, in a certain way. In a sense he was playing to the crowd.

We continued to explore and talk about these issues, and over the months, Graham would bring more examples of these situations to our conversations. This raised Graham's self-awareness of how these patterns of behaviour, which he had been mostly blind to, were happening with regularity.

This process, and our open exploration of these issues, made Graham start to feel more confident about these 'inspirations', and of how valuable they were. He also became conscious of exactly how much potential P&L this was costing him.

I finished working with Graham later that year. There then followed a gap of six years before I heard from him again. Then out of the blue, I had a call from him. He had phoned to thank me. "What for?" I asked.

He told me that over those six years he had become the trader he always felt he had the potential to be. He had more than doubled his average annual returns during those years.

THE HIDDEN TAX REVEALED

This chapter opened with the idea that failure to develop intuitive skills is a hidden tax on the trader's bottom line. Graham's follow-up gave me a chance to assess the cost of this hidden tax in his case. He ran $250m of capital. He was averaging around 4% return annually: about $10m. His compensation, after costs, was somewhere around 6%, about $600,000.

After the coaching Graham more than doubled his annual return. Sticking with the doubling figure, and since costs were fixed and knowing the structure of Graham's firm, his additional compensation on profits would have earned him about 10%. So for Graham this was personally worth about $1m extra annually. But, as his success grew, his capital allocation doubled, and since the extra income earned him 10%, the full extra benefit was $3m annually. This was the hidden tax which failure to develop his intuitive skills had been costing him each year.

And it was not just Graham who benefitted. He was now generating over $40m profit annually for his firm, compared to $10m previously. The lion's share of this went to their investors, but a large chunk went to the firm.

That is quite some hidden tax.

PART FOUR

THE PERFORMANCE PROCESS CYCLE – QUADRANT 3

CHAPTER 23

Meet Radical Uncertainty

Uncertainty is an uncomfortable position. But certainty is an absurd one.

Voltaire, author

T HE MODELS PRESENTED in this book aim to be useful, but they are not foolproof. Their shortcomings are summed up by statistician George Box, who said, "All models are wrong, but some are useful."

I find exceptions to the models and frameworks in this book regularly. That is the challenge of trying to simplify the complex.

To a Gestaltist, this is not problematic, but enlightening. These exceptions reveal something new, something interesting, something that needs exploring. They are openings. This is a Gestaltist's way of looking at things.

Gestaltism is the psychological approach which lies behind my coaching. When I learned to coach, I studied many different approaches, but it was the Gestalt method which struck me as most relevant to the world of financial markets.

Most coaching approaches seek to reduce an issue to a point at which it can be worked with. Gestalt coaching, by contrast, seeks to stay with the uncertainty. A Gestalt coach is encouraged to keep exploring and not to accept what they see as definitive.

Trading too is helped by a Gestaltist approach. When traders seek certainty, they are playing the ego's game. The ego wants certainty. It wants the sure thing, the win-win.

The sure thing is the seed of destruction which brought down Lehman Brothers and LTCM, and lies at the root of a million smaller trading failures. Not all trading losses are down to the search for the sure thing, but the search for the sure thing is behind almost all trading failures which result from catastrophic losses.

Trading requires embracing uncertainty, not seeking to escape it. But there is a particular type of uncertainty which is part of the trader's world: 'radical uncertainty'.

The term was coined by British economists John Kay and Mervyn King, the latter of whom served as the governor of the Bank of England through the 2008 Global Financial Crisis.

Kay and King distinguish between 'uncertainty', where cause and effect are knowable and therefore can be resolved, and 'radical uncertainty', where cause and effect are unknowable and impossible to discern and resolve.

Radical uncertainty presents a serious challenge to a person's ego. The ego hates uncertainty of all types and seeks certainty, but there cannot be certainty in a radically uncertain world. In the face of radical uncertainty, even the very best and smartest are fallible.

Isaac Newton, a genius in the purest sense of the word, fell foul of radical uncertainty in the markets during the 1720 South Sea Bubble.

Newton made a £7,000 profit on his first South Sea Bubble trade (that is around £1m in today's money). But after taking his profit he watched prices race higher, and heard of others making fortunes. Newton bought back in, at what turned out to be the top. He lost

£20,000 (around £3m in today's money), his entire fortune, when the South Sea Bubble collapsed. After that, he was reputed to have said, "I can calculate the motions of heavenly bodies, but not the madness of people."

THE RIGHT MAP

In Chapter 18 we talked about the pitfalls of carrying the wrong map, and how the map we have of the world in our head, informed by our education and culture, views problems through a complicated lens.

Radical uncertainty sees the world as complex or even chaotic. The difference between complex and complicated perspectives is best defined by how they interpret cause and effect.

In a complicated world, much like in Kay and King's conception of uncertainty, cause and effect can be discerned. Problems can be reduced to a formula which explains their working, and then solutions can be applied and repeated. The construction of a cardboard box, a cheesecake recipe, the design of a Ferrari engine, the guidance system of a rocket – all are complicated-world solutions. Once defined and solved, they are all repeatable. The same formula can be applied, and the same result will follow.

In a complex world, as with radical uncertainty, cause and effect cannot be discerned in real time. Sometimes they are opaque even in retrospect. The likelihood of a specific outcome will be based on forecasts or estimates driven by probabilistic assessments. As the number of variables increases, the possibility of accurate forecasts becomes increasingly remote.

A coin toss is a complex problem, though it sits close to the complicated boundary. There are only two possible outcomes. It is easy to reliably *predict the likelihood* of an outcome, but there is no *certainty* on any single coin toss.

Trying to predict where the S&P 500 index will close a year from now is an incredibly complex problem. The sheer number of variables needed to make even a remotely accurate estimate make it nothing more than a finger-in-the-air guess. If, for example, it sits at 3830, we could probably rule out it moving below 1000 or above 6000, but even then, the word 'probably' has to be used. We cannot guarantee either result with certainty.

All situations we face in financial markets require us to make an educated guess. Often even after they have occurred we may still not know they have happened, let alone their cause. Consider a 2002 IMF study which noted that, of 74 identified episodes of recession in different countries, only four had been correctly predicted by econometric forecasts published just three months prior to the recession year. In two-thirds of cases, consensus economists had failed to 'forecast' the recession even four months *after* it had started.

That's complex.

COMPLEXITY AND TRADING

In his book *The Behavioural Investor* (Harriman House, 2018), Daniel Crosby says that the only accurate equity forecast is: "I have no idea and neither does anyone else, but estimates don't provide lobster lunches and fail to meet our need for a belief in a knowable future."

Economists and analysts have to make forecasts in conditions of radical uncertainty. They often have to deal, unfairly, with flak from audiences of egos who want certainty. In some cases I've seen traders getting abusive towards analysts and forecasters on trading floors, using them as a punchball for their own failures.

Both these groups are considered to be specialists, but they are not performers in the same way traders are. They have the luxury of expressing their views without having financial 'skin in the game'.

Traders and investors are risk-takers. They do not have this same luxury. They have to perform and must have skin in the game.

Sam, an analyst on the challenging journey to portfolio manager once told me what had happened when she produced a forecast on a stock that had been underperforming.

She was given access to the company's c-suite board members and key stakeholders in their business, and also spoke with customers. She produced a thorough report, which she presented to the firm's portfolio managers. Sam said, "The report could not have been any more bearish if it had fur, paws, and answered to the name Yogi."

She fully expected any portfolio manager at their firm who held the stock to liquidate. But the following week, the senior portfolio manager at the firm had doubled his holdings.

This portfolio manager was considered a legend in the firm, and not someone you questioned. Sam managed to catch up with him in the coffee room the following week. Ironically, the portfolio manager said, "Nice report, some really good conclusions." She was even more baffled now, though she did not have the nerve to ask him why he had increased his position. "It was not for me to question him," she said.

Over the next three months, the stock rallied 10% from the low. Then after three more months, the senior portfolio manager liquidated fully. He did not just sell the additional holdings he had purchased, but his prior holdings too. Then over the next six months, the stock underwent a significant sell-off and reached new lows.

The context to this story is that we were exploring the difference between viewing the market as an analyst and being a risk-taker.

Sam asked me what I thought happened to make that portfolio manager act as he did, because she never fully understood it.

I explained that I could not possibly know, but I would hazard a guess that the portfolio manager probably agreed with her longer-term assessment. Nonetheless, as a risk-taker, he was assessing the sentiment of the market and the state of players in that stock. It sounded like the stock had sold off heavily in the run-up to her report. It was possible that in the portfolio manager's view the report confirmed what the market had now priced-in.

"But why do you think he went long?" she asked, adding "He could not have known the stock would bounce."

"Intuition," I replied. "I would guess he probably had an intuitive sense that in the short term the stock was as weak as it was going to get for now. Maybe he had seen heavy selling, which was struggling to push the stock lower. When that happens, it becomes a relatively cheap upside play. If you are wrong and support breaks, you can usually get out relatively quickly without too much of a loss, if the stock is liquid enough."

"And then?" she asked.

"If the market holds, some buyers return, and some shorts start taking profits. The stock then starts moving higher, then weak shorts get nervous and are forced to buy back, which triggers a reverse cascade effect. More weak shorts are then removed from the market, as they are forced to buy back. This happens until balance returns."

"So why do you think he sold when he did?"

"Again, I am guessing," I said, "but he may have agreed with your long-term view and felt this was as good a rebound as the market would allow."

The look on her face suggested a eureka moment had occurred. She said, "I now get why this trader always referred to a quote, which I understood in theory, but never quite fully realised the practical application of."

"Are you referring to the Benjamin Graham quote, by any chance?" I asked.

"Yep, that's the one," she replied snappily, before repeating the quote. "'In the short run, the market is a voting machine, but in the long run, it is a weighing machine.'"

THE TRADER'S EGO DILEMMA

Having to navigate radical uncertainty for a living is part of the game traders and investors play. They are not specialists in the markets, they are performers.

Many of the great traders I know place themselves in a state of not-knowing, so they can exercise and practise detached curiosity. Not-knowing is a challenging state for the ego, but great traders learn how to become comfortable with this discomfort.

Staying indifferent presents many challenges. A story from Nassim Taleb's *Fooled by Randomness* (Penguin, 2007), exemplifies this.

Taleb described how, when he was working as a trader at an investment bank, he was visited in New York by a friend of his father's. He describes the friend as "of the rich and confident variety." The father's friend wanted to pick Taleb's brains on markets.

Taleb preferred to see markets through the lens of "not having an opinion" (or not-knowing). Thus, as the friend of his father pushed Taleb for an opinion, he deflected, instead describing the nature of markets rather than expressing an opinion on them.

The exasperated friend eventually contacted Taleb's father, and said to him, "When I ask a lawyer a legal question, he answers me with courtesy and precision. When I ask a doctor a medical question, he gives me his opinion. No specialist ever gives me disrespect. Your insolent and conceited twenty-nine-year-old son is playing prima donna and refuses to answer me about the direction of the market."

The friend saw Taleb as a specialist, but Taleb was a performer. To the outsider, traders are seen as specialists, akin to a surgeon, lawyer, economist or analyst, but trading is a performance activity. No one accuses Roger Federer, or Beyoncé of being a specialist, they are considered performers, the same is true of traders, they do not know.

STRONG OPINIONS
LOOSELY HELD

As a trader progresses through the Being Phase of the Performance Process Cycle, they probe, sense and analyse a Trigger event that moves them to engage in sense-making. There may not be an obvious link between cause and effect, but nonetheless a picture starts to emerge which they are overlaying on to their own internal maps.

Holding a map which sees the world through the complicated lens leads to the map-reader seeking certainty. But any certainty created in this way is delusional and can get many a trader into trouble. Holding a map which sees the world through the complex lens allows the trader to embrace uncertainty. Traders who work in this way may form strong opinions, but they hold them loosely.

Traders love to quote an apocryphal line attributed to Keynes: "When the facts change, I change my mind. What do you do, sir?" But few traders are able to work in this way. One who could was George Soros. In *Fooled by Randomness*, Taleb says of Soros, "One of his strengths is that he revises his opinion, rather rapidly, without the slightest embarrassment."

TO THE RIGHT SIDE OF THE
PERFORMANCE PROCESS CYCLE

Everything we have covered before this point has related to the lefthand side of the cycle. But at the moment the trade is placed, the situation takes on a whole new dynamic for the trader.

Everything before this point has been the practice; now the performance begins.

CHAPTER 24

The Performance Phase

You don't have to be in a boxing ring to be a great fighter. As long as you are true to yourself, you will succeed in your fight for that in which you believe.

Muhammad Ali, boxer

WARREN BUFFETT HAS only referred to his Noah rule once. It was in his 2001 Berkshire Hathaway company report, following one of his worst years.

Buffett admitted that he had made mistakes that year. He had foreseen certain risks but had not converted thought into action. As such he had violated his Noah rule which states that 'predicting rain doesn't count; building arks does'.

The left side of the Performance Process Cycle is all about Buffett's rule. It begins with getting into an appropriate psychological, mental and physical stance for the battle which lies ahead. Then comes the groundwork: predicting whether, when, and how it will rain. Finally, an ark is built which can survive the storm.

When you deem the moment is right, you cross to the righthand side of the cycle, at which point you have to put your ark out on the stormy water. If it has been constructed well enough, it should survive.

During the ark's journey, you – as its captain – will find your mental and emotional capabilities stretched to the limit. You may not last the journey or reach your destination, but you need to survive so that you can go again.

The left side of the cycle, pre-storm, was the easy side. Most traders would grade themselves high in the abilities prioritised by the left side of the cycle. The righthand side is where the performance occurs, and this is where you will have full skin in the game.

Figure 28: The Performance Phase

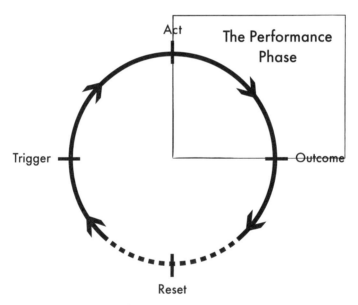

The Performance Phase is where the trader is most likely to be judged by their harshest critic: their self, inspired by their ego.

The trader's journey through the radical uncertainty of the Performance Phase misshapes and skews their perception. It will distort how they see their self, their world and reality. It unbalances their internal state, warps their perspective and drains their mental capital.

When this happens, their view and assessment of the external world becomes increasingly subjective and highly personal.

Their decision to act was made in the Production Phase, when they viewed the external world through a more objective lens. But in the Performance Phase the trade takes on a new character, with a different resonance and meaning for the trader.

There are many more self-inflicted problems which can contribute to behavioural slippage and undermine the trader's performance on the right side of the cycle.

The Performance Phase is highly traumatic. The trader will be acutely sensitive to threats and danger, causing their focus to narrow to the immediate vicinity of their activity, which potentially causes them to lose sight of the bigger picture.

They may trip over into fight, flight or freeze mode; making it difficult to stick to the plans their playbook requires.

Self-management, self-belief and self-trust are paramount in this phase.

It is on the right side of the cycle that the mental game baton is passed from mental capital to mental fortitude. The plan has been set and the trade readied. Now the trader has full skin in the game.

Mental fortitude describes the ability to remain present to our needs so that we can retain our mental capital, or at least some measure of it. It can be thought of as grit and resilience under pressure, so that we can still make optimal decisions and act appropriately in the moment. It could also be thought of as 'mental toughness'.

During the Being Phase and Production Phase, mental fortitude is not a primary requirement; but during the Performance Phase, as mental capital depletes, we will require mental fortitude to keep us from being overwhelmed by the slew of emotions our ego sends our way.

The trader must stay on-process; they must not have their agenda set for them by their ego and its purpose. They must stay true to their trading purpose. In short, they must remain in an optimal trader state.

The biggest danger for the trader is that in the midst of the Performance Phase their resilience evaporates, the red mist descends, and the trader is sent into a tilt state – in which every move is a wrong move.

The concept of achieving an optimal trader state may seem like high-minded idealism, but that is what outstanding performance demands. The ability to remain present is vital. The mental game can be won, if the trader can remain focused on facing markets and acting in accordance with what the situation demands, and if they can step back to see things with clarity and coherence.

THE PRODUCTIVITY PHASE AND THE MAY 2007 BUND TRADE

In Chapter 16 we saw that I had devised a pre-trade plan for how I would enter the Bund trade if the market gave me an opportunity. This included how much size I would risk, what the conditions would be for exiting if I was wrong, how I would add more if it moved in my direction, and then how I would trail and adjust a stop.

I knew that if I could get the trade on, and if it panned out the way I hoped, I was potentially looking at maybe a 4:1 or 5:1 return on this low-risk, high-reward setup. Though if I could get my size on smartly, it could be significantly better.

The first part of my act was to short the Bund future (equivalent to going long of yield) in accordance with my plan. My initial size was to be relatively small, and my stop quite close. I needed to be careful not to break the drawdown limit given to me by my employer, which I was not far from.

I started selling Bund futures.

I was not consciously thinking that this may be the asymmetric setup I had been looking for. I was just acting out the plan I had for this trade. My thinking had been done in the scenario planning of the production phase.

After I placed the first trade, the market rapidly moved in my favour. I quickly added more size, as per my plan, trailing the stop to keep the risk size the same.

Then the market movement started to gather pace, quickly reaching my third add level. I added again and trailed the stop, so my risk remained the same.

My risk of loss was never larger than the initial risk size, since I was recycling my profits and averaging in as I went along. I now had 60% of my full risk allocation on.

My risk allocation was set by the bank, using their very conservative Value at Risk (VaR) calculation.

The market continued moving my way, without abating. I added the final two tranches that afternoon.

I now had my full risk on, and still the market kept on motoring. I could now leave the stop further back since I was so far in the money.

As I had planned, at this point if the market corrected downward, stopping me out in the process, the worst that would happen was I would lose my initial risk.

I pushed for a risk limit increase. I was told I could use some of the unused option limit of our New York office, assuming I placed the trade in options, which I duly did, trailing the stop a little higher to cover this option risk.

Bunds closed on a low that day, a Friday, leaving the yield on a high of the day. My trade was significantly in the money. Even my stop level was significantly in the money.

That left me facing over the weekend risk, but my stop was far enough away that I considered this risk highly remote. On Monday, the market opened lower (yield higher) and continued moving in the same direction through Tuesday and Wednesday. I was now seven figures in the black, the move I had anticipated was on, and it had only moved about a third of the way towards my expected target.

Over the next three weeks the market continued my way, with barely a correction. As it did so, I continued to trail the stop. However, since the trade was now fully in the money, I had the luxury of relaxing the stop to allow room for some market volatility.

Eventually, as it approached my target level, I started letting go of the trade, booking the profit as per my plan.

I have never executed a more satisfying trade. I was in flow the whole way through. The return on the trade was a staggering 50:1. A true multi-bagger.

This trade was good to me; very good indeed. I grew an attachment to this trade. Only after exiting it did I experience my first stress and anxiety in relation to the trade. I will share this when we look at the final phase of the quadrant in Part Five.

CHAPTER 25

Win or Lose, Everybody Gets What They Want out of the Market

Win or lose, everybody gets what they want out of the market.
Some people seem to like to lose, so they win by losing money.

Ed Seykota, legendary trader featured in Market Wizards

THIS ENIGMATIC QUOTE comes from an interview with legendary trader Ed Seykota, in Jack Schwager's original *Market Wizards* (Wiley, 2012) book.

I have spent more time puzzling over this quote than any other words ever spoken about trading. When I first read them, I re-read them, then re-read them again. They made no sense to me, and yet intuitively I felt they were right.

I think I read that *Market Wizards* book three times in my trading career. Each time, I stopped at this quote and puzzled over it in the same way.

I have read many discussions of Seykota's words on various forums, and I guess everyone can interpret them in their own way, depending on their own perspectives and experiences. I will explain my own interpretation, which brings together many themes explored in this book.

MEETING OUR NEEDS

Psychologist Abraham Maslow identified five tiers of subconscious needs essential for a healthy and balanced life.

The bottom four tiers are needs that we may be deficient in: we cannot survive or live a psychologically healthy life without them. Working upwards, the first tier includes basic physiological needs which we require for safety and survival, including food, water, shelter, security, and protection. The next three tiers include things we get from human relationships. These include safety – things like employment, health and property; love – covering affection, companionship and friendship; and then the highest of the 'deficiency needs': self-esteem – which includes self-respect, self-approval and self-recognition.

In the ego-host-self metaphor, it is the job of our ego to ensure we act and behave in ways that enable us to meet these needs. If we suffer rejection, disapproval or exclusion then, in reverse order, the lower four needs are at risk of not being met.

These deficiency needs are things we will have craved from a young age. If we had not obtained them, we would probably not have made it to adulthood.

There is one further need, which sits atop the triangle (see Figure 29). This is known as 'self-actualisation'. It is not a deficiency need, but a 'being need'.

Figure 29: Maslow's hierarchy of needs

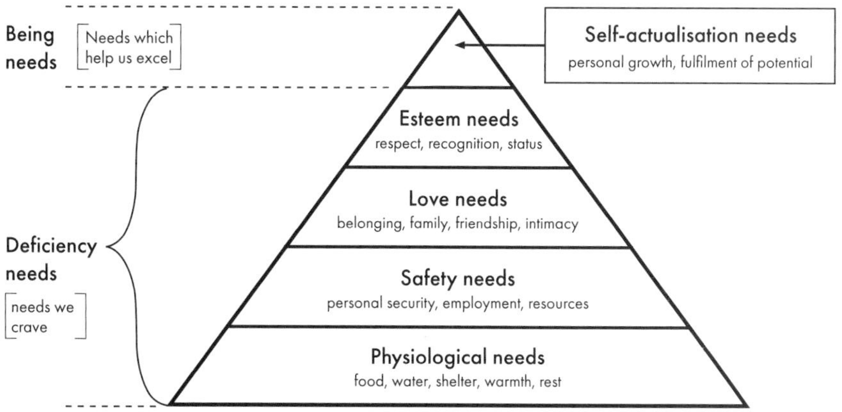

Self-actualisation is where we achieve our true potential.

When a person self-actualises, they accept who they are, what they are capable of, and they can more accurately perceive the world around them without judgement. They will therefore hold an accurate, rather than a warped, view of the world and their place within it.

People who self-actualise have a broader purpose, rather than attending to the wants which arise from unmet deficiency needs. They are likely to follow their own path rather than other people's. They will not be swayed by the crowd, but can read the crowd. They are comfortable in their own skin.

Self-actualisation is a state in which a person is freed from having to attend to their deficiency needs. Thus, they have a wider, broader, and deeper field of vision. They can stand back and look at problems with a fresh perspective.

When someone self-actualises, they can fully experience the wonders of life with humility, and they can celebrate those moments rather than let them pass them by. They can be their true self and bring the power of their true self to the moment.

Self-actualisation is an optimal state for the challenge a trader faces.

It is one in which they are comfortable not-knowing, where they can sit within discomfort, exercise detached curiosity and be creatively indifferent.

When a person self-actualises, opportunities come to them, and threats are dealt with. A person who self-actualises can bring their full mental capital to bear. They are truly present to their true self, their core purpose, and are not distracted by their ego-led purpose, which wants them to attend to deficiency needs.

WANTS: OUR UNMET NEEDS

Even when seeking self-actualisation, we must still attend to our deficiency needs. When we do not, our ego can become agitated. Once these are fulfilled to a sufficient level, we can then move on to pursue self-actualisation. But if we stay focused on our lower-level needs even when they have been sufficiently met, we may never realise self-actualisation. Thus our longer-term well-being is sacrificed at the altar of our short-term needs.

Consider one of our most basic needs: food. In the modern age, most of us have the food we need, but it does not stop us wanting more, and often we can become over-focused on fulfilling this need to the detriment of our well-being. As with so much that is part of how we behave, this has an evolutionary root.

Our ancestors did not have the luxury of an abundance of whatever they wanted, whenever they wanted it. Their human operating system encouraged them to overeat when they could, because they did not know when the next meal might come. It could be several days before their hunting and gathering provided further sufficient calories.

High-calorie foods were more prized than any other type. More 'energy bang for the buck' could be gained from foods naturally high in sugars.

We are now guided by the same human operating system as our

ancestors had then. Hence, our bulging waistlines. We are primed to overeat and to consume high-calorie foods, even though we know we have another meal coming.

The same is possibly true with the highest of our deficiency needs: self-esteem. In the same way we may be over-sensitised to the need for calories, we may be over-sensitised to the need for approval.

We worry about not having enough acclaim. We are acutely sensitive to a disapproving glance or remark. We fear our self-esteem evaporating as much as we fear mortal danger. In some cultures, death is preferred to a loss of self-esteem.

We even describe the behaviour of those who seek additional acclaim and approval as 'needy'.

Sometimes, our self-esteem needs can supplant lower-order needs. People want the respect of being seen as thin so much that they will starve themselves of the life-giving calories they need. Logic goes out the window. For these people there is no such thing as 'too thin'.

In this insanely complex world, with the increasingly fragile and inauthentic relationships we have, we crave the need to be liked and respected. People want to be followed on social media, and being unfollowed or ghosted can spark an existential crisis.

We all want the approval of our peers, even when we do not know them. We want people to love us, to say good things about us, to tell others about us, to go onto Amazon and give the books we write a 5-star review.

None of us are immune to this. At our core we all run on the same operating system.

Recall the new portfolio manager from Chapter 13, who featured in the story of the Hong Kong office of the hedge fund. She was the only one of her cohort of new portfolio managers and analysts who signed up for my coaching. I do wonder whether she would have followed up if she had attended the same meeting as the other portfolio managers and analysts.

Perhaps, by not being in that meeting, my soon-to-be-client's deficiency need for the approval of her peers was not triggered, and she could self-actualise. Certainly, she is one of the few from that group who is still at the firm, and she is by far the most successful.

It was possible that the other managers' deficiency need for the acclaim of their peers, allied to the belief that being seen to have help was a sign of weakness, stopped them asking for the help which could have benefitted them. Their egos came between their long-term well-being and the actions which could help them achieve that. The coaching may not have guaranteed success, but it would have increased the odds of them succeeding.

Still, in that moment, they got what they wanted. That was a personal win for each of them – in that moment.

Our wins, our short-term behaviours, fulfil a short-term ego need.

When we want food, we go for it and grab it. It is a small win at that moment. But often we do not need it. Thus, in the end we lose. We become overweight, unhealthy, tired, groggy. In the long run, we take in too much cholesterol, we suffer heart disease, diabetes and sometimes depression. To an external observer, it might seem as if we like to lose by continuing to chase small food wins.

We see this in so many aspects of life.

And it is the premise that informs my take on, "Win or lose, everybody gets what they want out of the market." Some people seem to like to lose, so they win by losing.

JUDGING SUCCESS

At the start of the Ed Seykota chapter in *Market Wizards*, Jack Schwager says that he knows of no other trader who had achieved what Seykota had in the time he had been trading. In a 16-year period, he had grown one trading account from $5,000 to $12,500,000. That is an increase of 250,000%. Had there not been withdrawals from it along the way, it would have been significantly larger.

The interview with Ed reveals a depth of wisdom which possibly surpasses that of any other interview in any of Schwager's *Market Wizards* books. Many of the answers Ed gives may seem enigmatic at a first glance, but a second or third read reveals hidden depths.

But it is the answer to Jack's final question which for me is the most revealing. Jack asked Ed how he judges success.

Seykota replied, "I don't judge success, I celebrate it. I think success has to do with finding and following one's calling regardless of financial gain."

I do not feel Seykota's trading success owed much to his analytical approach, system or method. There are probably a million failed traders who took identical steps. His success was down to him, the person.

Seykota had let go of the urge to satisfy his deficiency needs once they were met. He could then focus on his self-actualisation needs. This meant he could attend to his personal growth, self-improvement, ego-taming, humility, emotional self-management, continual learning, acceptance of not-knowing, embracing creative indifference, practising detached curiosity, and celebrating success.

CHAPTER 26

The Performance Effect

All the world's a stage, and all the men and women merely players.

William Shakespeare

I N EVERY GREAT performance there is a time, a moment, a fleeting second when you have to make a choice and act. You have immersed yourself in the role, done the practice, been through many experiences, and you now have to put yourself out there in full view of the world and allow the performance to happen.

Everything you've done until then – all your sensing, your scanning, your thinking, your analysis, your planning – goes into these moments. At these choice points, the decision is made to act; now the act must happen. Hesitation is as deadly as jumping the gun. You have to trust your self.

This is easy in theory, but very hard in practice. Why is it so hard to do?

THE TIGHTROPE ANALOGY

Imagine that you decide to learn to walk the tightrope – an activity not easy to learn, but one that with time, patience, persistence and a good teacher or mentor is achievable.

At the beginning of your training, the rope would be strung between two posts just a couple of feet above the ground.

As a novice tightrope walker, you would learn the basics of the art at a safe height. You would develop your balancing skills and techniques, foot placement, arm and body position, how to move forward.

After a while you would start to improve. At first, you move forward a little before losing your balance and taking a fall; but with time, you would become more accomplished.

Eventually you will make it all the way across the rope. Soon you will be going across the rope and then returning, at progressively faster speeds. Eventually you may even be able to do a few tricks.

I read somewhere that it takes about five minutes to learn and about one year until it feels totally natural, by which point you will be able to do some basic tricks. This is not totally unlike trading, in many ways.

Once you can cross a rope to a highly competent level, your teacher would start to move the rope higher – from two feet to five feet, then five feet to ten feet. Now things start to change. If you fall here, you fall hard and may suffer some serious injuries.

But what if your teacher then raises the rope to 100 feet: about the height of a ten-storey building?

In theory, the act of crossing the rope is the same whether it is at a height of two feet, ten feet or 100 feet. The technical aspects of tightrope walking are the same: foot placement, balance, body position. But, even if you wear a harness and have a safety net to catch you, it will never be the same at 100 feet. Your ego, which may have been relatively calm and quiet at the lower levels, is triggered at such heights, and your emotions will be jumping all over the place.

Up at 100 feet, you become fearful, anxious, nervous; you will possibly go into fight, flight or freeze mode at the slightest disturbance. Your focus will be on getting across and nothing else.

The tightrope analogy highlights the vast difference between taking risk in theory, when risk is low or non-existent, and taking it when there is far more on the line. When risk is very real, emotions are triggered and our ego takes over.

The ego is a bad trader, a bad performer, a bad actor. Instead it is your true self that you want to be doing the act. Your true self is the capable one.

THE FOMC MEETING DISASTER TRADE, AND MY REDEMPTION

2007 was a quite the trading year for me. After twenty years in my career, trading was still showing me that no amount of experience means that you stop making rookie errors.

I had my great Bund trade, then my mini-crisis of confidence that summer, from which I was saved by my colleague Ashley's intervention (as I covered in Chapter 1). But there was one more incident still to come.

After my conversation with Ashley, I started trading well again. My P&L was soon moving in the right direction.

However, in early November of that year, I did something that knocked me for six. The following is my recollection of these events.

I had positioned myself short of two-year yield going into the Federal Open Market Committee (FOMC) meeting at the end of October. The trade was placed using Eurodollar futures. I prefer using stops on my trades, but I remove these over highly volatile events, so that a momentary liquidity squeeze or vacuum do not take me out. Instead, I keep an eye on the position.

I was not expecting the Fed to cut rates, but to make a dovish statement which would indicate the possibility of future rate cuts had grown. This is exactly what transpired.

The market did not move much on this, and I felt very comfortable with the outcome. I placed the stop back on with my broker Justin, left my desk and went out to grab something to eat.

The stop I left was some way from the market price, and hence I felt no cause for concern.

As I walked back to my desk, I heard Justin shouting over my broker line: "Steve, are you there? I just want to check you heard that you were filled on your stop."

I rushed to my desk and said to Justin, "What do you mean, 'filled'?"

I looked at my screen. The yield was a few ticks higher than where I left, but not anything drastic. "Your stop was filled," he said.

"What? Where? How? What are you talking about?" I said, now becoming a blithering idiot, unable to string a sentence together.

I checked the price action on the short-term chart. The futures moved inverse to the yield, and made a quick 18-tick move lower, followed by a 10-tick return, while I was out of the building – a kind of very mini-flash-crash centred around the futures contract I was in. This had cost me a significant six-figure sum. I was fuming. I now had to think what to do.

My immediate thought was: "This does not change the big picture. The idea is still good, I must get it back on." But I hesitated. I don't know why – maybe I thought I would try another go at the level where I was stopped out. But the market did not return there. The futures moved higher again (the yield went lower) and were now 20 ticks (ten yield-basis points) from where I was stopped. (In those days each tick was half a basis point.)

Why didn't I just re-buy the position when I realised the error, rather than be 'a dick for a tick'? I asked myself.

I decided to leave it and try again in the morning. Perhaps the market would give me another opportunity to get long of futures near where I was stopped.

The next day I managed to completely screw that up. I again held off, thinking futures might come lower. But after a quiet European morning, they rallied from the New York open.

There was some data coming out. I feared this would send futures higher and I would miss out again. So I bought some futures ahead of the data. The data was strong, the futures sold off, yields bounced.

There are many swear words in the English language you can use in such a moment. I managed to use all of them.

I was now completely owned by this market.

"Why didn't you wait, you idiot?" my ego kept repeating on a loop inside my head. I think my self responded, saying, "You try and do better if you think you're so smart." The ego did not need a second invitation; it took the reins.

The ego squared the position. It managed to do so on the futures' low for the day. After that, the futures started rallying again. By the end of the day, the position I had taken pre-data would have been in the money.

When you are owned, you are screwed – that is it. You will do whatever the market wants you to do. It pulls the strings. You have no control over your actions.

The end of that week was a disaster. I had managed to give back all my gains of the past couple of months.

I was morose the entire weekend.

On the Monday and Tuesday, the futures rallied further. Like my May trade, I had called this well; but unlike my May trade, I completely screwed it up. Not only was I not in the trade, I had managed to lose money as well.

I could barely function in the early part of the following week, as I watched the market rip. It was now 40 basis points from where I was stopped. That is a huge move. I was spiralling. I could not see a right course of action, a way forward.

But then something happened that changed it all.

I picked up my journal, which was sitting on my desk, and opened it.

On the inside front cover of all my journals, I always paste a copy of the Rudyard Kipling poem 'If—'. I started reading through it.

> If you can keep your head when all about you
> Are losing theirs and blaming it on you,
> If you can trust yourself when all men doubt you,
> But make allowance for their doubting too;
> If you can wait and not be tired by waiting,
> Or being lied about, don't deal in lies,
> Or being hated, don't give way to hating,
> And yet don't look too good, nor talk too wise:

> If you can dream—and not make dreams your master;
> If you can think—and not make thoughts your aim;
> If you can meet with Triumph and Disaster
> And treat those two impostors just the same;
> If you can bear to hear the truth you've spoken
> Twisted by knaves to make a trap for fools,
> Or watch the things you gave your life to, broken,
> And stoop and build 'em up with worn-out tools:

If you can make one heap of all your winnings
And risk it on one turn of pitch-and-toss,
And lose, and start again at your beginnings
And never breathe a word about your loss;
If you can force your heart and nerve and sinew
To serve your turn long after they are gone,
And so hold on when there is nothing in you
Except the Will which says to them: 'Hold on!'

If you can talk with crowds and keep your virtue,
Or walk with Kings—nor lose the common touch,
If neither foes nor loving friends can hurt you,
If all men count with you, but none too much;
If you can fill the unforgiving minute
With sixty seconds' worth of distance run,
Yours is the Earth and everything that's in it,
And—which is more—you'll be a Man, my son!

At the end of that, I turned to the next free page in the journal and started writing.

Over the space of what felt like five minutes, I wrote three pages. I wrote what I felt, I wrote about my state, and then I started writing what my process is, what my purpose is, how I achieve my purpose, where I was, what had happened. A cascade of thoughts had come into my head, which I wrote out as they came.

After that, I suddenly felt clear. The clouds had all of a sudden lifted. Clarity returned. I had let go.

I recall saying to myself, "Right, now what are you thinking?"

The price action, the news, the data, the charts: to me, they all suggested that the move in yields had much further to go on the downside. Much more than I perhaps had originally considered. The risk-reward on this trade was excellent. But I had not been seeing it.

I had been acting as if I were on the tightrope, 100 feet up with no plan. I had become fearful, anxious, nervous. My focus was on survival and nothing else. But now clarity had returned.

I could see the trade.

"Ok, how much can I put on?" I asked myself.

That depended on where my stop would be if I was wrong. The market at these levels was uncharted territory, with no obvious stop point. I had to be creative and give myself an exit level. Once I had that, the next question was how much size would this allow me to place?

I acted. I got short of yield, long of futures. And I let it run.

Over the next three weeks, the market continued to move in my favour: yield dropped a further 70 basis points, adding well over seven figures of P&L into my book.

Returning to the question: why is it so hard to do in practice what we can do in theory?

In theory we should be able to walk a rope 100 feet off the ground in the same way we can walk a rope two feet off the ground. In practice, we cannot.

As the quote attributed to everyone from Einstein to Yogi Berra states, "In theory there is no difference between theory and practice, while in practice there is."

We are not robots. We are ego-driven, emotional beings, who are influenced by our relationships with others, our context and situation. We need to work with that, because we cannot fight it.

CHAPTER 27

Results Orientation vs Process Orientation

Some people want it to happen, some wish it would happen, others make it happen.

Michael Jordan

B RYAN CRANSTON WAS destined to be an actor. Born in Hollywood to showbusiness parents, Cranston decided early in his life that he wanted to follow in their footsteps. However, despite lots of promise, Cranston soon found his career was stuck, with him unable to land that breakthrough role in a big hit film or TV show.

In his autobiography Cranston talks about how he had got to a place early in his career where he was always hustling for work on commercials, landing guest roles in other people's shows and auditioning like crazy. He was making a decent living, but felt that his progress had stalled, as he called it, "in junior varsity." He was beginning to wonder if his career had reached a plateau and this was as good as it was going to get.

Fortunately, his wife took the initiative of buying Cranston some private sessions with Breck Costin, a renowned private coach in

Los Angeles who worked with high-performance individuals from various fields.

Costin suggested that Cranston focus on process rather than outcome. Instead of attending auditions with a view to win the role, he should go along with a view to giving a strong performance. Winning the role would be the outcome of this performance, rather than the outcome of an attempt to land the role.

This way Cranston could bring his best self to the audition. If he was right for the role, great, and if he was not, so be it.

This attitude broke the link between Cranston and his ego. He was no longer attached to the outcome of the audition and therefore to meeting an expectation. Expectations are often the work of the ego.

Cranston's new outlook was not merely a value he stated, it was something he fully espoused in practice. Outcome was now irrelevant. He no longer saw what he did as a means to an end, but as the end itself. The process mattered, not the outcome.

Once Cranston made the switch he felt free, and things started to change. He was no longer owned by the situations he was in; he owned his auditions and his space. He didn't always get the role, but that no longer bothered him, because if he did not land it, then he was not right for it

Shortly after this change, Cranston landed the role of Hal in the comedy series *Malcolm in the Middle*, a role he retained until the show's end in 2006 and which led to multiple award nominations for his performance. But this was just a stepping-stone to the sort of career-defining role which few actors ever achieve. Cranston was soon cast as the lead character, Walter White, in the blockbuster television series *Breaking Bad*. This show and Cranston's incredible acting skills were to give us some of the finest moments in television history. Cranston won multiple awards and honours for his brilliant performance, which was followed by a string of leading roles in TV, movies and theatre.

Cranston firmly credits his success to the switch to a process orientation, which enables him to work with purpose.

Maintaining focus on a process, in the face of a world which demands results, is incredibly challenging. All sorts of barriers and hurdles come at us, some from the environments and situations we are in, some from the expectations of others, and from our own expectations we pile on ourselves.

RESULTING

'Resulting' is a term which comes from poker and was brought to a wider audience by former poker player Annie Duke, author of *Thinking in Bets* (Penguin, 2018). Resulting is the tendency to evaluate the quality of our decisions based on the results they achieve.

When we 'result', we conclude that if we have a positive outcome, we made a good decision and followed a good process. Likewise, if we have a bad outcome, we conclude that we made a bad decision and must have followed a bad process.

In trading, the impact of resulting does not necessarily have to occur at the physical conclusion of the trade; we can often be in its thrall much earlier on.

The story of Tony and his Bitcoin trade in Chapter 9 provides a stark warning about the dangers of resulting.

Tony had a strong and successful process. On the Performance Process Cycle, Tony would have a trade plan at the execution point – the act. He would execute and then follow his playbook.

His simple Performance Process Cycle would look like Figure 30.

Figure 30: Tony's simple process

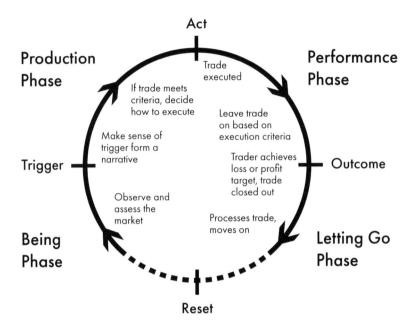

Now consider Tony's Bitcoin Trade. He was watching Bitcoin at $30,000, waiting for it to break its downtrend line. When it broke over $32,500, he had what he felt was potentially a 9:1 return trade. His stop was below $29,000. So, a risk of $3,500. His upside target was $65,000, a potential gain of $32,500.

If he was wrong, he would lose a set amount of his choosing. But if the trade worked, he would make close to ten times that. He would trail a stop, once certain levels were hit enabling him to reduce the risk, though potentially reducing the upside too. However, as his risk reduced, he could then add more risk.

Had he followed the plan, it would have worked perfectly. This is what his trade plan would have looked like on the Performance Process Cycle.

Figure 31: Tony's trade plan

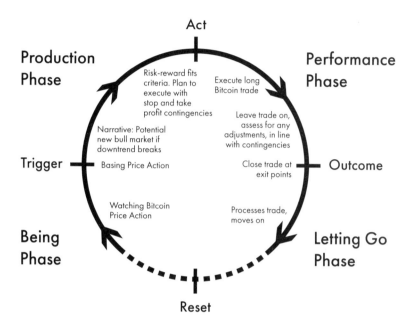

As Tony watched Bitcoin, somewhere along the line he felt he could do another Bitcoin trade.

Tony's playbook allowed him to make a second trade in Bitcoin, though this should have been a separate trade with its own Performance Process Cycle. That way, Tony's potential losses would have been limited by how much risk he had allocated to these two trades. In effect, Tony would have had two different long Bitcoin trades, each with their own criteria (though he would have aligned them). This had worked for Tony in the past. He allowed himself to have up to three trades on the same market.

But with the Bitcoin trade going so well, Tony decided to add to his first trade on a whim. He doubled its size. There was no planning, no process, no structure.

Figure 32 shows the effect of this action on Tony's cycle.

Figure 32: Tony adds to his trade

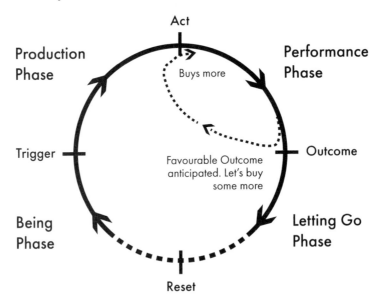

Tony had now started an unproductive cycle. He was off-process.

At this point the worst thing possible happened: Tony's gambit worked. Emboldened, Tony decided to try it again. He doubled up on his original doubling up of his size. And again, it worked. He was on a roll. He felt he could do no wrong, even managing to sell out and buy back in on a large dip in September. He was trading on whims, and it was working.

He was now fully spiralling in terms of his process, but because the results were good he was buoyed. It felt great.

But his unproductive process cycle was building. It was an accident waiting to happen, as Figure 33 demonstrates.

Figure 33: Tony's unproductive cycle

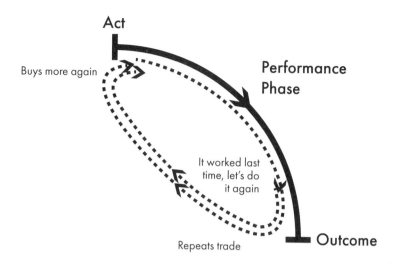

Tony described to me how he was "trading like a high-roller." He was following neither a player approach nor a house approach, but some strange hybrid of the two. It was all ego-led. His 3Ps triangle had been breached and looked like Figure 34.

Figure 34: Tony's 3Ps of High Performance

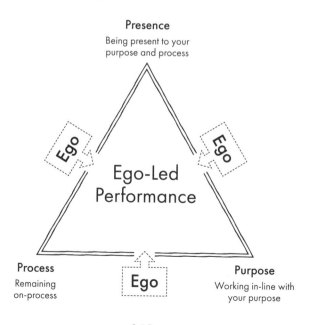

It was as if the casino had rolled out the red carpet for him, given him lines of credit, and as he made money they gave him more, and he used that again.

The house (and the market) wants you to spiral. Even when you are winning, as long as you are spiralling they can bank on winning it all back from you. In the moment you are winning, but you are owned.

Only by sticking to the original Performance Process Cycle, staying present to it and aligned with your purpose, do you stay in charge. Then you are owning, not being owned.

Resulting is pernicious. It happens below the radar. Tony slipped and allowed it to happen just once. Or so it seemed. As it turned out, this was not the first time Tony had done this. Until now he had always got away with it, or not suffered any serious damage. Each time, Tony told himself he would not do it again. But he could not help himself.

PROCESS ORIENTATION

I was drawn to Bryan Cranston's story by a headline: 'Ordinary People Focus on the Outcome. Extraordinary People Focus on the Process.'

High performers adhere to a process. Tennis players, boxers, athletes, musicians, comedians. They do their preparation outside the Performance Phase, so that when it comes around they can perform at their best.

All of the most successful traders I know owe their success to their process orientation: they adhere to the basic tenets of the Performance Process Cycle. With a process orientation they can bring the best of themselves to the market, whether they are house-approach traders or player-approach traders.

Once your mind jumps to thinking of the potential outcome of the trade and you take your eye off the process, that is when you start resulting. This is why trading is such a rollercoaster, able to pull you from feelings of despair to feelings of elation within seconds.

When the penny finally dropped for Tony, he said, "I know where and when I went wrong. I became obsessed with the outcome, when I should have been obsessed with the process."

From that moment Tony started to get closure on what had happened. When he came out with this statement, he said it without personal judgement or self-recrimination. It was as if he was talking about someone else. To paraphrase Winston Churchill, for Tony this was not the end, it was not even the beginning of the end; but it may have been the end of the beginning.

In a world obsessed with results, it is sometimes incredibly difficult to trust the process. But that is what the bargain you make with your self helps you to do.

Staying on-process, in the face of uncertainty and the constant agitation of the ego – with its tendency towards resulting – is a monumental task. It takes reserves of willpower and resilience which drain our mental capital.

The performance phase is about stepping out on to the stage ready, prepared, primed; and following your plan and strategy. This is what distinguishes the very best from everyone else, as Michael Jordan alludes to in the quote at the start of this chapter.

CHAPTER 28

Navigating the Performance Phase

The most we can hope for is to create the best possible conditions for success, then let go of the outcome. The ride is a lot more fun that way.

Phil Jackson, legendary basketball coach, led the Chicago Bulls and the LA Lakers to a combined 11 NBA championships.

DOUGLAS CORRIGAN WAS one of the last of adventurers and glory-seekers of the early days of aviation. He earned the nickname 'Wrong Way Corrigan' in 1938, when he claimed that due to cloud cover, he misread his compass and had flown from New York to Ireland instead of New York to California.

Reality may have been somewhat different; he had previously been denied permission to fly across the Atlantic to Dublin.

Corrigan's crossing, in a ramshackle airplane ill-suited to the demands of the journey, became the stuff of legends. The feat earned him hero status. He was given ticker-tape parades through the streets of New York and Chicago, and starred in a film celebrating his exploits.

A newspaper that reported his story described him as an aviator "who flies by the seat of his pants."

And so, the term to "fly by the seat of your pants", which means to trust your judgement and instincts as you go along, came into common parlance.

FLYING BY THE SEAT OF YOUR PANTS

When a trader goes off-process, they start flying by the seat of their pants – trying to do something without much practice or preparation. People who appear to do this often earn themselves legendary status. But the reality of their success is often very different. Usually they have done the preparation, and are in fact very accomplished at what they are doing. Wrong Way Corrigan was an accomplished pilot who had spent years preparing for that flight.

We often hear of traders who seem to have become overnight successes, but when you dig down there is a vast amount of planning, preparation and practice behind what they do.

Remember the firefighter captain who made the decision which saved the lives of his crew in Chapter 21. His decision was intuitive and instinctual, and though it was made in the heat of the moment (if you'll pardon the pun), it was also made on the back of over two decades of experiences.

When people see a comedian supposedly winging it on TV, with rapid one-liners and lightning-fast quips, they assume that person is a natural. But it is their commitment to practise, their dedication to learning, trying, failing and sacrificing over many years, which made looking natural possible. Steve Martin said, "I did stand-up comedy for 18 years. I spent ten years learning, four years refining, and four years as a wild success."

I know some brilliant traders who appear to go off-process, and to observers they may seem to be flying by the seat of their pants. But such a trader usually has a well-formed map in their head, a great understanding of the terrain, respect for the basic tenets of risk management, and still has their process behind them.

One of these traders, a seasoned house-approach trader delights in telling me how he goes 'off-piste' with his trading. But he has 30 years of experience and has earned the right to do so. He knows what he is doing. He is not flying by the seat of his pants, even if it feels to him like he is. He is a master improvisor. This is what accomplished house traders are, but it usually takes many years to become good enough to do this successfully.

Most traders do not know what to do when they start winging it. They do not have a process they can fall back on, or they cannot tell the difference between a process and hope.

SPENCER

One trader who fell foul of this was Spencer. He enjoyed trading by the seat of his pants.

Spencer was a former chef turned real estate salesman turned day trader. In the five years since he started trading, he had accumulated a decent track record. Then, in a few short weeks, it all went pear-shaped.

Spencer arranged a call with me to ask about my coaching. On the call he said, "Steve, I am long S&P, and it's killing me."

"Where did you go long?" I asked.

"4500," he replied. At the time, the S&P was trading around 3800.

He then added that he had only been looking for a small intraday move to somewhere around 4520.

He had been looking to make 20 ticks, and now was 700 points offside. "Holy moly," I thought.

"It's worse than that though," he said.

He initially placed the trade in his size, which was ten e-mini futures, but doubled up when it was 20 points against him.

A quick calculation in my head estimated that he was looking to make about $5,000 on the initial trade and was now down around $700,000.

I asked if he was able to furnish me with any more understanding of how this situation unfolded.

"It dropped quickly. I thought it was a short-term move and would come back. I was adamant that I was right to stay long. I've done this several times and it usually comes back."

After a brief pause, he added, "I was on a good winning streak, and I think I got a bit cocky, so I decided to double up at 4480. Then it just kept on going down. I'm a day trader, I take positions in and out quickly. Now I had a trade which was larger than I usually had, and it was way offside."

His emotions rose, his voice audibly changing as he carried on talking. "At the end of the day, I was holding this trade and I felt I couldn't get out, because it was just so stupid to get out at that level. So, I convinced myself that this was now going to be a longer-term trade. I told myself that the market was going to move back up to 4700."

This is a classic example of the endowment theory cognitive bias. Spencer gave a greater value to the S&P trade he had because he was already long of it. The view he had was because he was long, not because he thought it was a good trade. He was now hope-trading. When you hope-trade, you are pretty much owned.

Then he went on. "Now, months later, I am still holding the trade. It is costing me a fortune and I can't function. I can't sleep, I can't trade, I can't even think straight."

Spencer was traumatised. He had burned through all of his 2020, 2021 and 2022 profits. He had also burned through his initial trading capital and was now selling assets and taking loans to stay in the trade.

He told me how on many occasions he had gone to pull the plug on this trade, but he could not bear to consider the amount of regret he would face if he cut and then saw it rip higher. I asked him why he didn't cut out now.

"Because I know it will be the low," he replied. "And besides, I need to make the losses back."

Spencer was trapped, and completely owned.

Spencer's experience is symptomatic of the challenge of trading. Irrespective of whether you are a day trader, a longer-term trader, a market-maker, an investor, someone who is largely systematic or completely discretionary, the battle within your self *is* the battle.

BE COMFORTABLE BEING UNCOMFORTABLE

Navigating the Performance Phase is a white-knuckle ride riven with dangers. If you start winging it and are not skilled or experienced enough to do so, if you engage in flights of fancy, and if you do not have a robust risk framework behind you, there will be a price to pay at some point. Spencer was paying his.

The Performance Phase is where the quality of your relationship with your self will be tested more than anywhere else. Sometimes we can have a relationship with our self that is beset by self-doubt, but sometimes we can overvalue our self and have too much confidence. Spencer was in the latter group. His inner game was antifragile; it was too rigid. Our inner games need to be able to bend and absorb. When something is too rigid, it can appear strong; but in the face of too much weight, it will fracture and snap.

Being willing to be vulnerable, makes it possible to 'be comfortable being uncomfortable'. This is a vital quality for traders, particularly in the Performance phase. This does not mean showing that you are not hurt – that is where your ego comes in. Instead it requires you to be willing to appear vulnerable, as Muhammad Ali did in his preparation and in his fight against George Foreman.

When sports psychologist Damian Hughes was on the AlphaMind Podcast, he described the way in which world heavyweight boxing champion Tyson Fury is a master of this. When Fury is knocked down he takes the full count to get back up, whereas the mistake many boxers make is to spring upright straight away. They want to show they are not hurt.

What these boxers do is the worst thing in that situation. A boxer who tries to show they are not hurt actually becomes more vulnerable. In these moments, Fury maintains the 3Ps of High Performance: he remains fully present to his purpose, which is to win the fight; and to his process, which requires him to take the full count. Fury uses every second available to gather his thoughts, restore his balance, reset and ensure he can return to the fight in the best possible state.

Fury can improvise like the best of them. That is what great performers do. But at key moments he does not fly by the seat of his pants; he resorts to process. That is the difference between winners and the rest.

CHAPTER 29

Staying Positive When the Market Wants You to Be Negative

Never let the fear of striking out keep you from playing the game.

Babe Ruth

YOU CANNOT GET away from losses, errors and bad outcomes in trading; they are part of trader's terrain. How you learn to handle them is what matters, not whether you have them.

Earlier I talked about what the market wants for you. I made the point that trading is like a giant poker game. You can either lose by luck, or you can lose because your ego undermines your ability to play well, causing you to make mistakes and eventually sending you on-tilt.

That is what the market wants. It is what the market *needs*. Its purpose is to take your money. While your purpose is to take money from it.

There is a saying used in military circles: "Never interrupt your enemy when he is making a mistake."

The market is not going to do anything to help you. It allows you to make mistakes, then twists the knife, as it did for Tony and Spencer.

If you are like most traders, you then end up doing everything you can to help the market get its wish. That is not your fault, your human nature functions that way. Recall that our ego is not a flaw or a bug, it is a feature.

Our tendency towards resulting allows the ego in. When we have a good outcome, the ego encourages us to get carried away. The result is that we usually end up giving that money back to the market.

When we have bad outcomes, we end up resulting the other way. We either go into denial and delude our self into thinking that it will come back, as Spencer did; or we internalise bad outcomes and undermine our self by destroying our own confidence and self-belief.

When this happens to you, your presence weakens until the trinity of the 3Ps is breached. Your presence usually goes first, followed swiftly by the abandonment of your adherence to your purpose, and the collapse of your process, finally followed out the door by your physical capital.

Learning how to handle negative outcomes in order to succeed is a vital element of trading. Getting better at being uncomfortable is a mental ability, not a physical one.

This requires the development of mental fortitude. Tony Robbins describes mental fortitude as containing four key elements:

1. Challenge: seeing hardship as opportunities.

2. Confidence: eliminating self-doubt.

3. Commitment: never giving up.

4. Control: taking ownership of your destiny.

These are more than mere catchphrases. There is substance behind these elements. Many people just see these headlines and build their mindset based on them, never looking deeper.

MIND GAMES

Many people resort to mind games when they trade. We all have our personal tricks which help us get through, but most people use them to disguise the flaws in their process.

Spencer tried mindfulness, meditation and positive reinforcement. He was a big fan of Tony Robbins and attended his shows almost religiously. But this did not help Spencer, because his process was flawed. His trading was an accident waiting to happen. Playing these games only masked his flaws.

It does not matter how good or well-structured your process is, drawdowns and setbacks happen. That is the nature of working in radical uncertainty. Every house-approach trader will periodically suffer a large drawdown or a series of smaller drawdowns that accumulate. That is not a failure, it is meant to happen.

The same is true for player-approach traders. They will suffer periods of bleed, missed opportunities and erratic returns.

When these setbacks occur, no one will be immune to the negative feelings, which can dent your confidence and undermine your presence. That is what allows the ego in. Then ego-led performance follows.

Spencer was not afraid of a challenge, but when Robbins talks about seeing hardship as opportunities, he means seeing setbacks as a chance to regroup, learn from your mistakes and forge ahead. Spencer could not accept setbacks, which made him vulnerable. He fought back rather than stepping back and assessing.

Spencer never gave himself room for self-doubt; he believed in Robbins's mantra for eliminating it. But Robbins talks about doing this by becoming better at being uncomfortable, allowing failure to be an option that you can live with – much like Cranston did.

'Never give up' does not mean stubbornly fighting against an enemy bigger than you. It means finding a way to win. Ali could not beat

Foreman by going toe-to-toe with him, so he found another way to beat him.

Because of Spencer's misinterpretation of Robbins's message, he was not taking ownership of his destiny, but was owned.

TRIPWIRES: A PERSONAL RISK MANAGEMENT TOOL

I have referred several times to 'tripwires'. In this sense a tripwire is a concept I was introduced to by sports psychologist Damian Hughes, one of the world's leading experts on cultivating a high-performance mindset, when he was a guest on the AlphaMind Podcast with myself and Mark Randall.

A tripwire is a tool or mechanism we have handy for when matters take a turn for the worse. Often we will be blind to the need to stop, check and change things, because we are working on autopilot. A tripwire is an alarm that goes off when things change beyond what is acceptable. It is designed to limit exposure to risk.

The term was originally coined by the band Van Halen. Their tripwire was a clause in their performance contract that stated the venue must provide a bowl of M&Ms with all the brown M&Ms removed. To the organisers at the venue, this probably seemed like rock diva behaviour. To Van Halen, it was a vital part of their prep.

Upon arriving at the venue, the band members would check out the M&M bowl. If there were any brown M&Ms it meant that the organisers had not been thorough in their preparations for the show. They then knew that they had to do a thorough check of all aspects of the production.

In the episode Hughes told us how we can all introduce tripwires into our lives at key moments. He shared a story of a time when he was working with world number one squash player James Willstrop.

Willstrop had one opponent who always seemed to create momentum against him, which would then disturb Willstrop's ability to play his own game. Hughes told how they came up with a tripwire for when this happened, which involved Willstrop untying and retying his shoelaces three times.

As a player-approach trader, I had to survive the long periods between winning trades and the bleed which accompanied them. But this could play havoc with my ability to remain in an optimal state. To help me I had a mantra which became a tripwire. I would remind myself that good trades were like London buses: they may not arrive on time, but they always come along eventually, and sometimes more than one at a time.

I had other mantras which served me as tripwires. "Learn to Love Your Losses," which I mentioned earlier, was one I would use when I was starting to get risk averse. It reminded me that I needed to have losses in order to win, and not to see risks as things to be avoided. This way I was more accepting of taking and running risk.

Another was: "Next 1000 trades." I would bring my attention to this as a reminder that trading is a process, and that my last trade and my next trade were not as important as I thought they were. It was the aggregation of trades over my entire process that mattered.

As we saw in Chapter 26, I would also read the poem 'If—' during low moments. This tripwire worked as a grounding mechanism.

STRESS: PHYSICAL AND MENTAL WELL-BEING

You – as a whole – are the engine of your trading; you in your entirety need to be as optimal as possible. The Performance Phase is challenging for all traders. Retaining physical and mental balance is a key objective which can support you through its duration.

Trading is a highly stressful activity that will eat away at your mind, body and soul. Stress disrupts the healthy functioning of the mind, agitating your ego, which leads to a sharp increase in anxiety and heightened emotions. This then reduces your mental capital, erodes your mental fortitude and piles on ever more stress.

This can and does have consequences on your physical heath, your mental health and your key life relationships. These consequences then reflexively impact your performance.

All performance activites – including trading – require mind, body and soul. Therefore, every edge you can get counts. Activities which support mental, physical and personal wellness should be seen as vital parts of your trading process.

Keeping your nutrition and hydration optimal are vital for good mental balance, as is a good sleep regimen. Many traders use sleep-tracking rings and avoid too much screen time. Some even wear blue, light-blocking glasses.

Regular physical exercise should also be part of your routine. I used to enjoy breaking up my day with a run around some of London's amazing parks. Some of my best trading ideas would come to me on these runs, when my head was clear of any baggage, noise and clutter.

Likewise, having your personal life, financial matters and relationships as settled and ordered as possible can also enable you to maintain higher levels of mental fortitude.

There can be value in outsourcing peripheral aspects of your other interests, so that they do not become a drag on your ability to bring the best of your self to your performance.

Being enclosed in a small physical space, day after day, is also unhelpful. As is being isolated and alone. Trading is a lonely job; we need interactions with others. Try to develop social relationships which can break the isolation; preferably physical ones, but if not via audio or video communications.

Your mind and body need space and time away from screens. This is one of the benefits of running or walking – an opportunity to clear the head.

Finally, there are activities designed to tune in your mental health and improve your mental well-being. These include yoga, mindfulness and meditation techniques which aim to restore balance and calm, preparing you for the day ahead or replenishing these elements during the day. Many top traders work with professional instructors for this reason. The benefits of yoga include:

- Improving your concentration.

- Creating a calmer, more relaxed mind.

- Preparing you to face stress.

- Helping you step back from the fray.

- Enabling you to let go of bad outcomes.

- Giving you time to think.

As we reach the concluding section of the book, the focus shifts towards the concept of Letting Go. While we have touched on this subject multiple times already, the themes explored in the Performance highlight examples of Letting Go in a subtle manner. I firmly believe that having the ability to Let Go is what will ultimately carry you to success in any game. Therefore, this final section will dive deeper into this essential skill, providing you with valuable insights that illuminate the art and value of Letting Go.

PART FIVE

THE PERFORMANCE PROCESS CYCLE – QUADRANT 4

CHAPTER 30

Letting Go –
A Superpower

The best way of preparing for the future is to take good care of the present, because we know that if the present is made up of the past, then the future will be made up of the present. All we need to be responsible for is the present moment. Only the present is within our reach. To care for the present is to care for the future.

Thich Nhat Hanh – Vietnamese Zen Master,
Buddhist monk, teacher, and peace activist.

W E ARE NOW at the fourth and final quadrant of the Performance Process Cycle. Before I take you through this stage, I want to share a story about a remarkable trader called Lisette, whom I had the pleasure to coach near the start of my coaching career.

Lisette worked on the bond desk of a US investment bank. She was one of several traders in a programme, and over the next few months she and I were to have some fascinating chats about her work as a trader.

During these chats Lisette revealed she was a talented poker player, regularly travelling to Las Vegas and Atlantic City. She had a terrific track record and had occasionally gone toe-to-toe with some of the biggest names on the professional circuit.

For Lisette, poker and trading were synonymous. The games were different in detail, but the philosophy she applied to them was the same. In an attempt to help Lisette find out more about herself, I thought I would explore the less multidimensional world of poker, since it was probable that some of the same factors could be applied to her trading.

I asked her what she thought was the differentiator between her and most other players she crossed swords with. She pondered this question for a bit, then replied, "I'm not sure, I've never really thought about it at that depth."

The question had her stumped, and she went into a period of deep reflection. A few minutes passed, then she said, "I'm really not sure, Steve." A moment later she continued sheepishly, "Maybe it's that I walk away better than most people."

"What does that mean?" I asked.

"Well, after a bad night, I leave the table and can quickly put whatever happened behind me."

She said that her husband had made her aware of this. He played poker too, and on several occasions had remarked how well she seemed to be able to move on from a bad night. For him, on the other hand, bad outcomes played over and over in his mind.

Lisette said that she had not really been aware that this was an edge, but as she thought about it she started to suspect it might be. She had seen how her husband's inability to exorcise the mental baggage from a bad outcome in a previous game came to weigh on him in future games.

When that happens to a player, she told me, you start playing hands you should not and start placing bets randomly. That is when you start leaving money on the table.

After a short pause, she added, "Come to think of it, I don't just walk away from the night better than most people; I walk away from most hands better, so maybe it applies *during* games too."

The conversation was now starting to flow. I pushed her for more. "Do you have any specific examples of this," I asked.

"Yes, absolutely." She leaned forward and asked me, "Do you know how hard it is to fold a full house?" She did not wait for my answer. "I have seen entire careers ruined because players folded a strong hand which would have won a huge pot. Some players never recover from that."

She was in flow now.

"It's not the loss of money or the foregone pot that does the damage, it's the ego-hit, and the player's inability to accept what happened. They cannot put it behind them. The regret of that hand is carried around with them like a heavy sack on their back. Their ego is severely bruised, their ability to trust themselves in the moment is torn to shreds. They are so full of regret, anger and remorse that they abandon all reason. They start changing their game, they forget the structure which underlies their process, they refuse to fold when they should, then they start spiralling out of control. Slowly at first, but then it gathers pace in the weeks and months that follow."

She paused, and let the pause hang in the air, before adding, "You see, I can fold a strong hand that should have won, realise that I was played by an opponent, and live with it." She paused again. "And that is what I did in my trading too. I can screw-up and not be owned by it."

"Do you not feel the pain?" I asked her.

"Yes, I'm no stranger to the painful emotions which go with that. It's horrendous. You try to hide your pain, but no one can be emotionless in the face of that. You have to put distance between yourself and what happened. You mustn't let it change you and how you subsequently act."

Lisette had me intrigued. I asked her how she created this distance.

She told me of a time she recently folded a hand she would have won. She had a strong flush but folded when she thought she was beaten by her opponent, who turned out to be bluffing. This was someone she had not played with before, and she could not get a read on him. "It was very painful, and I was disturbed," she said.

She played on for a bit, but she was no good after that, so after a few more rounds she extricated herself from the game.

The next day she tried to process what had happened. "I reminded myself that this is a game, that there is luck involved, good and bad, and that sometimes bad outcomes happen that you can't control. It's not a reflection on me. I asked myself: in the same situation, with the same limited information of the player, and given how he was playing, would I do the same thing again?"

"And would you?" I asked.

"In that case, I think almost certainly, yes. For me and my process, it was the right thing to do. If I'd had a stronger read on him, it may not have been. But, not knowing his game well, I was right to fold, because that is what my process requires. 95% of the time my process is right. Abandoning my process is infinitely worse than one or two bad outcomes."

"What about if, on reflection, you'd realised that you should not have done that?" I asked.

"Well, I would have learned something new. And with that, I would have been happy, got closure on it, accepted what happened, been grateful for the learning opportunity, let go, then moved on."

Lisette smiled at me, again leaned forward, and said, "I would have done the same whether I won or lost."

"What do you mean by that?" I asked.

"What if I do something stupid and win? Should I be high-fiving myself? No, absolutely not. I try to process all my big hands in my head at the end of the night. If I think I should not have done something but it still won, I will make a mental note not to repeat that. I got away with something I should not have done. If I did something stupid and lost, I am grateful for the defeat, because I should not have won. I get a lesson, make a note of it, and then move on. But it's only a lesson if you heed it, otherwise you will repeat it. And when you repeat it is when you start struggling to let go, because you become blind to it. It can become a habitual error."

Before I could respond, Lisette said, "On second thoughts, perhaps in saying I 'walk away' better than most people, I used the wrong phrase. I think I should have said that I 'let go'. I don't think I'm better than other poker players in any other part of the game, but my ability to let go is where I come out on top. And I do exactly the same in my trading."

There you have it. In that one exchange with Lisette, it dawned on me that the ability to let go is where, more than anywhere else, the mental game is won.

CHAPTER 31

Letting Go

Between stimulus and response there is a space. In that space is our power to choose our response. In our response lies our growth and our freedom.

Viktor Frankl, Man's Search For Meaning

T HE MARKET DOES not want you to be able to let go. The market will do everything in its power to stop you being able to let go. It will toy with you, tease you, play games with you, mess with your mind, let you think you are winning, screw you up totally, then spit you out penniless, if it can.

The market is merciless.

Physical closure is easy; it is a transaction. Mental closure is something else. Tony got physical closure when he exited his Bitcoin trade, but he did not have mental closure.

The opposite of 'letting go' is 'holding on'. My clients, Tony and Spencer, were holding on to something. When you hold on you are attached, and when you are attached you are owned.

The ability to let go is not just the greatest skill a trader can have, it is the most under-appreciated skill of trading.

Figure 35: The Letting Go Phase

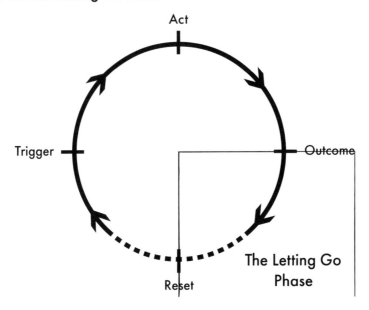

In the Being Phase, the importance of detached curiosity was emphasised. Attachments to ideas, narratives, beliefs, your ego, your rightness and your need to know all reduce your ability to exercise detached curiosity.

During the trader's journey around the cycle, and particularly through the Performance Phase, the trader's emotional pressure gauge becomes elevated as their ego gets increasingly agitated. As this happens their mental capital depletes, their mental fortitude erodes and their ability to function effectively and make good decisions becomes compromised.

After a trade the trader needs to release this pressure, reset and return to a balanced state so that they can replenish their mental capital and function effectively in the next cycle.

When the trader fails to rebalance, they bypass the Being Phase on their next circuit and enter a sub-optimal process cycle, which precedes the process of spiralling and potentially entering the dreaded trader's death spiral. If this is not recognised and exited, sub-par performance and performance destruction follow.

It is letting go which gets a trader out of this negative cycle. This is why it is a Power zone. This ability, probably more than any other, more than your analytical ability, your method, your system, your ability to react, intuit, improvise, your levels of market intelligence and know-how, more than any other, is the delineator of sustained success.

And yet, the Letting Go quadrant of the cycle is the one that usually gets the least attention in the trading process. It is, however, highly valued by exceptional traders, who devote energy and attention to this phase, like Lisette did in the last chapter. For her, it was her ability to let go that was the differentiator between her high performance and the lower performance of others. She competed against poker players far better capitalised than her, far more experienced than her, who were able to devote near-total game time to poker, and yet she was regularly matching them when she clearly had no right to do so.

As Viktor Frankl says, in the space between stimulus (the outcome) and how we respond, lies our freedom to choose. Tony had lost his freedom to choose his response when the key moment came. By contrast, Lisette ensured she retained the freedom to choose her response.

When a person does not let go, they become stuck. They cannot move on, they cannot move past, they cannot release, they cannot own. They can only be owned.

CLOSURE AND ACCEPTANCE

Whether a trader is satisfied by the outcome in the Performance Phase should not matter at this point. What matters is whether they can get closure on what happened, accept it, put a line under it, let go and move on.

When they do, they enter a space of nothingness; this is the 'Fertile Void'.

The Fertile Void is the area at the bottom of the circle, represented by the dotted or dashed line.

In one sense this place is empty, yet in another it is rich and nutritious. The mind, body and soul have been weakened, disturbed, sapped by the journey around the cycle. The trader's energy and precious mental capital have been depleted. The Fertile Void is where they heal, where balance is restored, where energy returns and where growth takes place.

The Fertile Void can be seen as analogous to a fallow field. The purpose of allowing a field to lie fallow is to allow the land to recover, to store up life-giving organic matter while retaining moisture and disrupting pest lifecycles and soil-borne pathogens.

In the Performance Process Cycle, The Fertile Void is a place where attachments have been left behind. No energy is directed towards the previous narrative, the sustaining of the ego or the retention of old beliefs or views.

When the trader passes through the Fertile Void, they have left all of that behind and can start afresh. They can return to their core purpose, get back to sensing and awareness and practise detached curiosity. They can start again.

This process also allows for learning. The memory of events gets stored and the lessons for our experiences are incorporated into who we are. We can then adapt as we learn.

THE LETTING GO PHASE AND THE MAY 2007 BUND TRADE

In 2007 I closed my Bund trade out with a significant profit. Things could not have gone any better.

But bizarrely, I soon found myself getting agitated as I watched the market continue moving lower (and yields moving higher). For the first time since I placed this trade, I started to have negative feelings and to doubt myself.

The market continued moving in the same direction, and if anything the pace which it moved at increased. I now felt pain and angst. Part of me wanted to go back in and re-enter the trade, but another part of me was resisting. These two parts of me are the key to the distress I felt. My ego was questioning and challenging me. It demanded more, and as it did so it was causing me to doubt myself.

I cannot say for definite what may have caused this, but an incident along the way may have been a factor.

Let's go back to the story from Nassim Taleb's *Fooled by Randomness*, in which the exasperated friend of his father pushed young Taleb for an opinion. Taleb deflected, instead describing the nature of markets, rather than expressing an opinion on them. He had wanted to stay neutral on the market; he did not want that neutrality to be compromised by being forced to express an opinion.

A week after I placed my trade, a similar incident occurred to me. I was asked by a senior manager and the head of risk to explain why I was running such a large position. I was not in breach of any limits at this point, but I think they may have been slightly unnerved and wanted to cover their own backs, just in case it went wrong.

I felt I should come up with a rational explanation. I could not talk about the finer aspects of technical analysis, volume, sentiment, Fibonacci extensions, momentum and my intuitive sensing, since I knew from previous discussions that these concepts were largely alien to them, it was like talking a different language. So I had to construct a narrative that sounded convincing and would keep them satisfied

This narrative described how sentiment data was detecting a pick-up in economic activity, which may lead to an increase in inflation. I told them how this was impacting the bond market and driving curve steepening in both the US and Europe.

I sounded like a CNBC scriptwriter. I did not subscribe to any of that; if anything I subscribed to a fundamental narrative that was the complete opposite. But since this trade was not based on a fundamental narrative, that was not relevant.

But now, as the trade was closed out physically, I recall grabbing onto this narrative as a reason to potentially get long the yield.

I still ponder as to why I became so agitated at this point. I wonder if it was because this trade had been so good for me, it had satisfied my ego and my ego had gained an attachment to the trade, and now wanted more. I had physically closed the trade; but I had not got mental closure.

I had the ego saying to me, "If this moves a lot more, you'll kick yourself. You had it on, and you missed it. See, you're not so smart after all."

This struggle continued over the next two weeks, as the market repeated another 50% more of the move that I had captured.

I knew at a conscious level that I should not re-enter; I knew I was not in an ideal state, that I would be owned by the market and trading without a plan. But the ego part of myself was desperately trying to take over and place the trade, and the ego is a dreadful trader.

I resisted, and eventually the market started to pull back. For a while I felt better. But then, after a correction, the yield took off again. Of course, the ego resumed its diatribe. I still had not got mental closure on this trade.

Eventually, the market did roll over; and as it did, I started to feel better about myself. The pressure eased. Eventually I got closure and was finally able to let go.

But for two to three weeks, this drained my energy. I was in conflict with my ego, which is exhausting.

Recall that the market has an agenda: it wants your money. To get it, it first convinces you that you can take money from it. Then, when you try, it relies on you spiralling and unravelling. That is what the market wants for you.

The market wanted me to unravel. It was relying on me to unravel. But, I did not go back into the market. In fact, I avoided taking any trades during this period. I was not in a state to make sound judgements. Instead, I let go, that was not in the market's plan for me.

I navigated the Letting Go Phase well in the end, but not perfectly. I would give myself a five or six out of ten, which is far better than earlier in my career, when I would have managed a two or three out of ten at best.

I believe that only the rare, exceptional traders can achieve seven or eight out of ten with regularity when it comes to letting go. These traders are the masters.

Many of the themes relevant to the Letting Go Phase have been covered indirectly as we have progressed through the phases of the Performance Process Cycle. In many ways, the entire book has been about letting go.

For the next few chapters, we will cover themes with practical applications that will help you in your fight to master the mental game of trading.

CHAPTER 32

The Reset – Entering the Fertile Void

It is not enough that we do our best; sometimes we must do what is required.

Winston Churchill

FOR ALMOST TWO months, I had been trying to set up a follow-up call with Eduardo, a retail trading client. Eduardo was based in Yonkers, New York, where he traded equity futures. He started trading in the early 2000s, initially as a side hustle to his work as a software data engineer. But after a couple of years, he was bitten by the trading bug and started committing to it more seriously.

While many individuals have the potential to earn income through trading, few are able to do so on a level that truly replaces the security of traditional income sources, particularly in the early years where more emphasis should be on learning, and where income is likely to be patchy or non-existent, and where losses are a regular occurrence. Fortunately, Eduardo had the advantage of an additional income stream from consulting which afforded him the time to develop his trading ability and allowed him to survive the early years until his trading started providing a stable source of income, and start building additional capital.

2009 was Eduardo's breakthrough year. Ever since then he had consistently produced a profit, and though results were highly variable they always cleared a minimum threshold he set for himself.

Eduardo still had the benefit of some small but additional income from his part-time consulting work. His wife also earned a decent income, which added some extra security, particularly when they began a family.

We started working together in late 2018. The previous year had been challenging for Eduardo. It was his wife, who worked as a psychotherapist, who suggested to him that working with a coach might be helpful.

During our time together I gained huge respect for Eduardo's high-energy approach to trading. However, here we were in the third quarter of 2019, and he had gone quiet. When clients go quiet, it is often a sign that they are not in a good place.

After several attempts to reach Eduardo by email, he eventually replied. He apologised and said he had just been so busy that he forgot to respond. We put a time in the calendar for a couple of weeks later.

When we eventually did have our videocall, I could tell by his voice and demeanour that things were not good.

"Oh, Man," he said, shaking his head. "It's been rough. I can't tell you how much I've messed up."

I was aware that at the end of June he had been doing really well. He was up around $500,000, which was more than double his previous year's entire profit.

"Steve, you're not going to believe it," he said, as if he was trying to avoid telling me exactly what had happened.

"Go on," I said.

He steadied himself, then started to tell me.

He had gone long of a stock in June. It rallied well, and feeling confident, he added some more. He was sitting pretty. Then, at the end of July, it snapped, suddenly breaking sharply lower. He did not panic, instead using the correction to buy some more. The stock held in at first, and some good trading around its sell-off meant that he was only slightly underwater on this stock, while still holding his core position in it. Then one day, just before the market opened, a trader on a chat group said he had heard that a significant analyst was calling the stock much lower over the next couple of weeks.

Getting a little emotional, Eduardo said, "I disagreed with that view, but it made me nervous. Then from the open the market started to move lower. I was getting increasingly uncomfortable, so I decided to pull the plug and exit the trade, even though it was nowhere near where my stop was. But you know what the market did then?"

It did not take a rocket scientist to guess. "It bounced?" I responded.

"Yeah, too right," he said in his thick New York brogue. "But it didn't just bounce; it soared. Within a few days, I would have been booking a big six-figure profit. Instead, I had taken a $50,000 loss on this trade, and I'm feeling like a complete idiot."

He sighed and continued. "I was so angry that I allowed that news story to throw me off guard. So, I decided to get back in. No plan though. I got long at the point where I would have been taking profit had I held the trade and not sold. Then the next day it trades up again and I have made most of the loss back, feeling good about this, I added some more, but I still didn't have a plan. Then some news about the company hits the wires, and boom! It dumps. But I am not having this, so I buy some more as it dumps. Don't ask me why, I thought I was better than the market. It was like I thought I could hold back the sell-off singlehandedly. Can you imagine that? Little me, trading from my basement in Yonkers?"

He was now getting agitated. Something was coming I sensed.

"But the worst thing that could have happened, happened. It ignored this news and moved higher. My ego was on fire, now. I was on top of this tiger, I could smell blood. I decided to go for the jugular and so I added some more. What made me do it, I do not know. I was already beyond the max size I allow myself."

He paused for breath. "Then, it just turned. It was like it was waiting for me to just buy that last extra lot, and as soon as I did, as soon as I made that one final mistake, it collapsed. And it carried on collapsing and I now am getting carried out. In two days, on this trade, I dropped half a mill."

"Since then, I have traded every move as bad as you could possibly trade it. And I've given back another $100,000. That's why I couldn't reply to your emails. I was in a hole and couldn't get out. The more I tried, the worse it got."

In a few weeks he had gone from $500,000 up to $100,000 down and was seriously spiralling.

Eduardo had gone off-process. He had a bad outcome from this initial trade, but rather than getting closure, accepting what had happened and moving on, he let his frustration get the better of him. He started revenge trading. That strange phenomena whereby we start taking revenge on our self.

He did not reset. He did not return to the Being Phase and try to get back to an optimal trader state. Unprepared, out of balance, with no self-control, no plan, he rushed back into the market.

He was owned. Totally owned!

Figure 36 shows what happens when a trader short-circuits the Performance Process Cycle as Eduardo had done.

Figure 36: Short-circuiting the Cycle

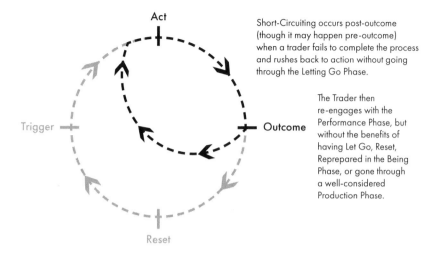

Short-Circuiting occurs post-outcome (though it may happen pre-outcome) when a trader fails to complete the process and rushes back to action without going through the Letting Go Phase.

The Trader then re-engages with the Performance Phase, but without the benefits of having Let Go, Reset, Reprepared in the Being Phase, or gone through a well-considered Production Phase.

This left Eduardo in a sub-optimal trader state. His ego now had its grubby hands on his trading. He was not relying on a solid or robust process, or on his usual ways of working. He was winging it.

Eduardo entered a downward spiral, beginning a vicious cycle of behaviour which fed on itself.

The situation deteriorated until Eduardo was finally in the trader's death spiral.

Figure 37: The Trader's Death Spiral.

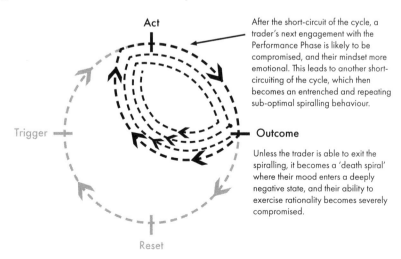

After the short-circuit of the cycle, a trader's next engagement with the Performance Phase is likely to be compromised, and their mindset more emotional. This leads to another short-circuiting of the cycle, which then becomes an entrenched and repeating sub-optimal spiralling behaviour.

Outcome

Unless the trader is able to exit the spiralling, it becomes a 'death spiral' where their mood enters a deeply negative state, and their ability to exercise rationality becomes severely compromised.

The only way to escape this was to start engaging with the Letting Go process.

We can also view this spiralling on a wave chart of the Performance Process Cycle, together with Eduardo's P&L as the spiral occurred, in Figure 38.

Figure 38: Eduardo's Performance Process Cycle as a series of waves, with spiralling

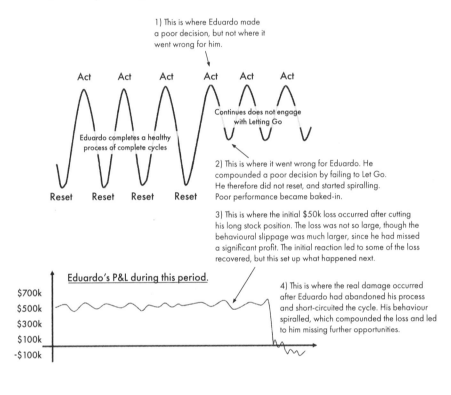

1) This is where Eduardo made a poor decision, but not where it went wrong for him.

Act Act Act Act Act Act

Continues does not engage with Letting Go

Eduardo completes a healthy process of complete cycles

Reset Reset Reset Reset

2) This is where it went wrong for Eduardo. He compounded a poor decision by failing to Let Go. He therefore did not reset, and started spiralling. Poor performance became baked-in.

3) This is where the initial $50k loss occurred after cutting his long stock position. The loss was not so large, though the behavioural slippage was much larger, since he had missed a significant profit. The initial reaction led to some of the loss recovered, but this set up what happened next.

Eduardo's P&L during this period.

$700k
$500k
$300k
$100k
-$100k

4) This is where the real damage occurred after Eduardo had abandoned his process and short-circuited the cycle. His behaviour spiralled, which compounded the loss and led to him missing further opportunities.

The initial loss from the bad decision at (1) was not the problem even though this was a setback. Bad outcomes happen.

It was Eduardo allowing this setback to get to him that became the problem. He made the mistake of rushing back in. He did not reset, ground himself, let go. The real failure happened at (2).

Point (3) on Eduardo's P&L chart shows the initial setback. (The real setback, behavioural slippage, was larger because he had foregone

284

potential profit). But the failure to Let Go took him off-process, there was an initial rebound in P&L, but he was now off-process, and this was the seed of the performance destruction which was to follow at (4).

Now let's consider how this may have looked in a parallel universe, had Eduardo let go of the initial error after just a single loop of the spiral.

Figure 39 is the same spiral on a wave chart of the Performance Process Cycle, together with Eduardo's P&L, but this time Eduardo only goes off-process for one sub-optimal spiral, then let's go.

Figure 39: Eduardo's Performance Process Cycle as a series of waves if he had Let Go after the first short-circuiting

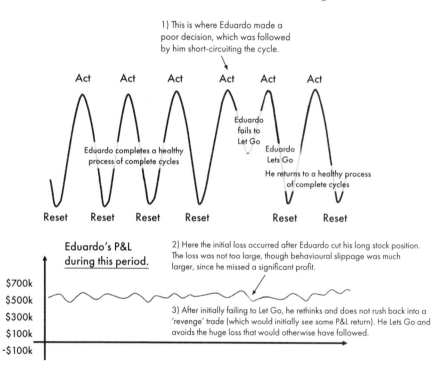

As you can see, damage is limited here. Instead of the large subsequent loss, which occurred at (4) in Figure 38, Eduardo lets go and balance is restored. Eduardo's mental capital is replenished, and he can get back on with following his trading process.

THE PRIMARY, SECONDARY AND TERTIARY IMPACT

The failure to let go has three impacts separate from the original error.

The primary impact is going completely off-process and allowing the ego to take over the trading.

The secondary impact is the poor trading which follows. This may be accompanied by hope-trading, revenge-trading, ill-discipline, FOMO and many other poor trading behaviours. After the big hit Eduardo suffered, he went into a period of sub-optimal trading, which added a further loss.

The third or tertiary impact can't easily be quantified in an image. Eduardo lost his confidence. He engaged in beating himself up. He was riven by self-doubt, in much the same way Tony was after his Bitcoin loss. Fortunately, Eduardo's hurt was not as deep as Tony's.

After his final $100,000 loss, Eduardo stepped away from trading for two weeks. During that time we explored this issue in a couple of coaching sessions. After that he felt ready to start again. He reduced his size initially, enabling him to return to presence. His process was fine, he just needed to restore his self-confidence and self-belief.

There was still some work to do. Eduardo stressed that his goal was to make his money back. This was a red flag. Recovering his losses was an ego-led goal, one that could take him off-process. We talked about following his purpose and setting goals connected to that, rather than chasing outcomes.

Eduardo set purpose-led goals for the final three months of the year which were achievable but slightly stretched. Stretch goals keep you pushing your boundaries; being too comfortable is also counterproductive.

His confidence quickly returned. He re-established his size within a couple of weeks and managed to finish the year well, outperforming the stretch goals he set for himself.

Healthy completion of a Performance Process Cycle is vital for trading success. When healthy completion happens, the trader passes through the Fertile Void, in which they regenerate and re-energise.

In this story, Eduardo spent two weeks getting closure, letting go and spending time in the Fertile Void. His energy was restored, he returned to balance, he checked in with his purpose and revisited his process. He knew what he had to do, and he started doing it.

CHAPTER 33

Self Compassion – Soft Power

A man cannot be comfortable without his own approval.

Mark Twain, author

I N HIS INTERVIEW for *Unknown Market Wizards*, Amrit Sall tells of an incident where his keyboard froze during a European Central Bank meeting. Amrit had just shorted the euro when the ECB president, Mario Draghi, made a comment which required him to immediately reverse the trade and go long. But with his keyboard frozen, the extra few seconds of delay ended up costing him almost a quarter of his trading capital.

You might have expected Amrit to go into a deep sulk, to start lashing out, perhaps to react with fury. But instead he went out with a few friends to a bar that night and had what he called "a celebration."

In his words, "What could I do? I realised that I could either accept it and move on or let it affect me emotionally in ways that were not going to serve me well. I put it behind me as quickly as I could. We had what I call a celebration because I wanted to shift my focus to the positive aspects of my situation rather than sulk over my loss. I was grateful to be in a position that offered so much potential for earnings."

Amrit was practising self-compassion. He ensured he did what Eduardo should ideally have done after suffering an initial large loss. Rather than letting it own or define him, his ability to exercise self-compassion ensured he could quickly let go and get back into his trading. Within a week he had recovered the huge loss from the day of the ECB.

TRADING IS A TRAUMATIC EXPERIENCE

The radical uncertainty of markets, and the necessity of facing the unknown on a daily basis, often brings us face to face with our inner demons.

My coaching conversations often get to a place where people, either consciously or unconsciously, share some aspects of their inner demons. People often talk of hearing a voice whisper that they are no good and will never amount to anything.

These insecurities and doubts often emerge just when we least need them, when we need our composure. They are the work of our ego, and their impact is to compromise our presence, which allows the ego to hijack our process.

My own experience with these voices found that they played a part in creating self-doubt, just prior to the trade. They would make me anxious, nervous and fidgety during the trade. Then they would lead to me beating myself up after it.

The doubting kept me from fully seizing opportunities. If I took trades and they succeeded, my ego would make me feel I was the beneficiary of luck. If I took them and failed, it was proof that I was not cut out for success. Sometimes my inner demons would keep me from taking a trade because I felt it would probably fail.

When I hit bad runs, this was merely the proof which reinforced what a loser or failure I was.

I am grateful for the indirect interventions of colleagues and managers at key moments. The incident with Ashley and another one of a similar nature when I was a trader at Credit Suisse, with the head of trading there, Sadeq, gave me reassurance when I was in a dark place and losing money, stand out for me. These incidents indicate the soft power of compassion.

I was not able to see myself spiralling on these occasions. But, as I have witnessed with countless other traders, once you are in that spiralling place, it is incredibly hard to see yourself with the objectivity you need at that point to exit the spiral.

When this happens, the trader starts to swear and cuss. They kick the desk. The phone gets smashed down. A stream of profanities flows from their mouths as they throw insults at their broker, analyst, junior or whoever they want to blame for their own failings. Whoever phones them gets short, sharp, angry responses. This can carry on for hours, days, weeks.

Their colleagues do not consider talking to them, because they are not approachable, and they know they won't be thanked for it. But whatever trade they are in, it is almost a sure thing that it is only going to get worse while they are in it.

The ability to exercise self-compassion is a powerful one.

The parallel-universe scenario I described for Eduardo is what I experienced in my November 2007 trade following the FOMC meeting in Chapter 26. It took me a little longer than Amrit to exercise self-compassion, but once I did, I let go and ended up making a considerable trading profit.

Self-compassion is simply the ability to be kind to yourself. It has immense power.

Mohammed Ali showed self-compassion when his team wanted to

remove his sparring partner from the training camp. Ali was good to himself at that point, and that ultimately helped him beat Foreman. Success lay not only in the hard power of his punch but also in the soft power of self-compassion.

Self-compassion is the ego tamer. The ego can make us loathe our self, dislike our self, beat our self up. It will bring up all the failures and rejections of our past, and our other inner demons, to aid it in its cause. It will set impossible expectations for us, then get us to berate our self when we do not achieve them. But self-compassion is a power we can use to push back.

Being more self-aware, checking in with our self, being conscious of our state and developing the art of self-compassion as a practice has real value.

Self-compassion is empowering. It enables you to let go, so that you are not owned. Instead, you own your journey.

But it will not happen on its own. It is against our human nature to react in the way Amrit did. He said himself, "As a trader, you are continually going up against your own emotional limitations. That is why so few people succeed in trading."

The refrain I always hear from traders is, "I am my own worst enemy." To combat this, you have to become your own best ally.

CHAPTER 34

Developing Your Human Potential

You'll get more from a £900,000 rider with a coach than you would from a £1m rider without one.

David Brailsford, manager of Team Sky cycling team

TEAM SKY, THE British cycling team, was formed in 2009. Until then, in over 100 years, no British rider had won any of the three major Grand Tour events, which include the Tour de France. Team Sky's ambition was to provide the first British winner of a Grand Tour event within five years of its inception.

They provided the first British winner the very next season.

Over the subsequent seven years, British riders dominated the Grand Tour, winning the Tour de France six times out of seven.

Team Sky's success was down to fully embracing the Human Potential Movement. Though they had a significant budget, it was not the budget's size that mattered but how they used it. They did not merely throw more money at the team, they changed the focus of investment. Whereas at the time over 90% of a typical cycling team's investment went on cyclist salaries, Team Sky reduced this to 80% and then progressively lower. They put the remainder of their financial resources into investments in coaches, non-riding staff, research and training camps.

Team Sky were the beneficiaries of the legacy of a similar move adopted by the British Olympic movement.

In the 1996 Olympic Games, Great Britain finished 36th in the medal table with only a single gold medal. After that, Britain went about building a programme for select sports, which saw the development of new facilities, the application of sports science and a strong focus on personal coaching. The results saw a stunning turnaround. Britain finished tenth in the 2000 medals table, with 11 Gold medals. Since 2008 it has finished in the top four at every Summer Olympics.

The Human Potential Movement has permeated almost all areas of high performance, including sports, music, dance, drama, martial arts, special forces military, senior business leadership, entrepreneurship, the field of medicine and surgery. The bigger the prize, the more the performers embrace coaching as a means of improving performance.

However, the Human Potential Movement has barely touched the world of trading and investment. Here the idea of performance coaching is considered anathema by many. In most high-performance fields, people fall over themselves to work with coaches and to go through performance and behavioural assessment. In the world of trading and investment, the opposite happens.

There are a few exceptions, and I have worked with some of them, but outside of these, human potential development remains on the margins. Banks and funds invest billions every year on data, tech, and research, while spending somewhere not far north of zero on developing their talent. What investment there is, is usually knowledge focused.

I have mentioned the reluctance of many traders to engage with personal performance development. They feel it would be an affront to their pride. The world of professional sports saw a similar response in the early days of embracing performance coaching.

The NBA coach Pete Newell was retained by the LA Lakers in the early 1970s to help develop players' specific skills. But, as sportswriter David Halberstam wrote in his 1981 book *The Breaks of the Game* (Hachette, 2009), NBA players didn't want to admit they "still had something to learn."

This started to change when LA Lakers player Kermit Washington approached Newell for private one-to-one tuition.

Washington, a big defensive forward, had been drafted by the Lakers in 1973. But he played only sparingly in his first three seasons and was getting progressively less court time.

Washington had realised his game was not as strong as it could be. In college, his size and athleticism allowed him to dominate smaller and weaker players, but these advantages disappeared in the professional arena. Realising that his lack of skill was catching up with him and his career was going backwards before it had truly got off the ground, Washington decided to take positive action.

His decision to approach Newell was unique in the pro-sports world of that time. After working for just a few months with Newell, Washington improved in every aspect of his game and was soon a regular starter. He went on to have a long and successful career, though one that was marred at times by controversy.

As other players noticed Washington's huge improvement, they also started working with Newell. Over the next few years Newell was to work with some of the legends of the game, including Shaquille O'Neal, Hakeem Olajuwon, Bill Walton, and Scottie Pippen.

In an article written for the *New Yorker* magazine, James Surowiecki credits Washington's initiative as being the first mover in bringing the performance revolution to the world of sport. Surowiecki said:

> Professional athletes had always worked out, of course. But, historically, practice was mainly about getting in shape and learning to play with your teammates. It was not about

mastering skills. People figured that either you had those skills or you did not.

That sink-or-swim mentality remains pervasive in the world of finance, which is not aided by the secrecy within the industry.

As a result traders chase the holy grail of system, method and knowledge. But these are rarely where the edge lies. The edge is within the trader.

The MIT blackjack team did not just put their system to work, they took a professional approach to personal development and individual performance. Kaplan only agreed to back Massar's team if it was run as a business with formal management procedures, a required counting and betting system, strict training, player approval processes and careful tracking of all performance.

Some players were averse to the idea. They had no interest in being put through trial-by-fire tryout procedures before being approved to play. They objected to being supervised in the casinos and having to fill out detailed player sheets after every session. Those individuals never made the cut.

Performance development and performance monitoring in the trading industry rarely get serious attention. The exceptions are, as usual, the exceptional performers.

WHAT LOOKS NATURAL
RARELY IS

Tom Dante's tale from Chapter 15, concerning the successful prop trader who stayed behind to complete his review late in the evening, reminds us of how those who excel go against the grain. They put in the hard yards and travel that extra mile in order to make things that are difficult seem easy.

Michael Jordan was not the best teenage basketball player in the world; he was not even the best basketball player in his college. But Jordan worked hard to become better. He maintained an intense work ethic and strong desire to become a better player, both then and throughout his career. A former college teammate, James Worthy, told how Jordan would continue to practise after the rest of his teammates were ready to go home.

The largest, and one of the most successful, hedge funds of all time follows these same principles. Bridgewater Associates is built around a culture which has many similarities to that of the MIT blackjack team. Started by Ray Dalio, who became an advocate of the Human Potential movement, the culture cultivated and the principles espoused by Bridgewater became the secret sauce underlying the firm's success. One might have thought others would try to imitate it, but so far they have not.

American psychologist Bob Kegan wrote of Bridgewater:

> Bridgewater stands for the pursuit of what is true, no matter how inconvenient, both as a business necessity in the financial markets and as a path for personal evolution and cultural integrity.

Many people scoff at Bridgewater's culture, finding it too challenging. But there is a reason it has become the world's largest hedge fund.

Another firm which has embraced human potential is Mike Bellafiore's proprietary trading firm SMB capital, based in New York. Employing the services of renowned trading coach Dr Brett Steenbarger, SMB has proved to be one of the most successful and enduring proprietary trading businesses.

It is clear that successful trading demands exceptional performance, underscoring the need to prioritise the development of human potential to maximise returns. Despite this pressing need, it begs the question: why has the financial market industry been slow in adopting the key principles of the Human Potential Movement, especially given the huge amounts of capital at stake?

I will suggest a few reasons why I think this may be.

1. LACK OF HARD DATA ON THE BENEFITS OF HUMAN PERFORMANCE DEVELOPMENT

In a results-driven business, people always want the hard data, but there is barely any to support the benefits of performance development. The best we have is anecdotal evidence.

Cory Mitchell, a trader who also coaches traders on the technical aspects of trading, analysed the success rate of traders at the proprietary trading firm he worked at. This is not audited scientific data, but largely anecdotal private research. His numbers seem to match very closely to my own anecdotal assessments and are not far from other anecdotal research assessments I have read.

Looking at day traders, out of around 2000 Mitchell analysed only about 4% were able to make a living from day trading. Some 10–15% were able to make money but were not earning enough to sustain a living.

One of the huge benefits of working in a proprietary trading firm is having experienced traders around who you can ask for advice, feedback, and help. Cory stated that hardly any of those who failed took advantage of this. One prop trading client suggested to me he believes that, with a good mentor in a prop firm, a trader's likelihood of success doubles. Getting help remains the domain of the extremely successful.

Once again: getting help remains the domain of the extremely successful.

2. SHORT-TERMISM, AND AN UNWILLINGNESS TO COMMIT TO PERFORMANCE DEVELOPMENT

The industry, as well as being results-orientated, is famed for being short-termist.

Personal and performance development does not produce an instant tangible win. Managers prefer fad ideas and new hires. Committing to develop your number-one asset, your people, requires a long-term commitment to performance development.

In addition, in most trading businesses, personal development activities are delegated to a learning and development department or an HR team. Even though these professionals are highly skilled, their primary focus is on managerial, executive, and general employee development, rather than individual traders and investors.

While I have worked on a small number of staff development projects for banks, these were arranged by individual managers taking the initiative to improve their teams. They never had the commitment of the banks behind them. When the manager left, all interest in personal development ended.

3. VIEWING TRADING AS A TRANSACTIONAL AND INTELLECTUAL ACTIVITY, NOT A PERFORMANCE ACTIVITY

The industry is obsessed with finding the edge in data, systems and knowledge. These are all vital ingredients. This is understandable, and yet if you have followed the red thread which runs through this book, you have probably grasped that human performance is the biggest edge available in trading.

The idea that the most academic or intellectual candidates will make the best traders runs counter to much of the anecdotal evidence on what makes a great performer in trading, investing and leadership.

The red thread which holds this book together, and which sees significant outperformance in trading and investment, is people's mastery of the mental game. I have known many highly intellectual people who have achieved great success in trading, but I believe it was their mastery of the mental game, rather than their intellect, that was the differentiator.

4. MORE THAN JUST LEARNING

Most trading firms quite rightly provide courses and learning programmes for new traders. Banks and funds provide graduate learning programmes but not performance development. Other than the coaching I was offered as an experiment, I never had a single day's training or development while I was a trader. From what I understand, not a lot has changed in the 22 years since then. Graduate programmes are not substitutes for performance development.

I do understand that trading is best learned experientially. I agree with that, but then so are cycling, boxing, guitar, basketball, mountain climbing. I was an amateur even after 13 years in the job. Then I had coaching. Coaching is beyond learning and beyond the transactional.

In sport, the higher people go the more coaching they have. In most performance fields, the same is true. In trading, it is almost completely absent.

5. MISUNDERSTANDING OF WHAT PERFORMANCE COACHING IS

The term coaching has become so generic that often it is difficult to understand how a coach can help. If someone were to suggest working with a coach, you would probably think of someone who will teach you a new trading system or method rather than working on you as a person.

A performance coach is different. As my colleague at the AlphaMind Project Mark Randall said, coaching is about making you a better you; so that you become a better trader. It focuses on you and how you execute your process, rather than the process itself.

There are relatively few true performance coaches in the world of trading and investment who are sufficiently qualified and have sufficient knowledge and experience to coach effectively. The lack of demand for coaching and performance development has probably created this vacuum.

These are just the main reasons why I think the Human Potential Movement has eluded the world of finance. There are many more. It does seem bizarre that, in a multi-trillion-dollar industry, so little is done to develop talent.

CHAPTER 35

Becoming Your Best Ally

Most of us spend too much time on what is urgent and not enough time on what is important.

Stephen Covey

B ECOMING YOUR BEST ally requires you to do something extra, something different, not to just follow the usual tried-and-trodden path.

Amongst my clients are traders and portfolio managers who are, and who have been, at the top of their game. 'Good', for them, is not good enough; nor is 'great'. They want to become elite, and stay that way. To achieve this they do something different: they engage with coaching and other activities to get better, to move towards becoming elite. That is what exceptional performers do.

When Team Sky achieved outsize success, it focused on the productivity of its cyclists, not just on hiring the best cyclists and giving them the best equipment. They wanted their cyclists, individually and as a team, to become elite. Kermit Washington did something similar. Instead of following the course he was on and hoping for some sort of turnaround, or merely allowing nature to take its course, he got active. He focused on how he could be more productive as a player. He became elite.

Becoming elite must be the aim of every trader. Even if you fall short, you will be far further along the journey than you would have otherwise achieved.

There are many things you can do, but only you can do them. You need to take ownership of you, your trading, your journey, and to do that you have to become your best ally.

Earlier in the book I talked about the advantages of making your playbook and your bargain with yourself explicit, the benefits of journalling, the power of developing tripwires and of engaging with coaching in its various forms. These are some of the many things you can do to boost your productivity and effectiveness.

This entire book is built around the concept of the Performance Process Cycle and its application to trading. The Performance Process Cycle is also a productivity tool. Many traders I work with assess themselves against the cycle and explore their trading in relation to its various stages. Some keep a copy of it handy and visible, as a reminder to themselves. I have made a copy available at performanceprocesscycle. com which can be copied or printed out.

In this chapter I would like to provide some more simple and easily adapted tools which can help you focus on being more productive as a trader.

The framework consists of a simple two-by-two matrix: two rows and two columns. You label the two columns 'things that are urgent' and 'things that are not urgent'. You then label the two rows 'things that are important' and 'things that are not important'.

You then have a matrix which looks like Figure 40.

Figure 40: Covey's matrix

	Things that are Urgent	Things that are Not Urgent
Things that are Important	Box 1	Box 2
Things that are Not Important	Box 3	Box 4

You then categorise all the tasks you do or should do in your work.

BOX 1: THINGS THAT ARE URGENT AND IMPORTANT

Box 1 should contain all the things that are imperative in your work. This can include following the market, the news, analysing data, getting research, doing analysis, generating ideas, following your system and risk management, among other things.

BOX 2: THINGS THAT ARE NOT URGENT AND IMPORTANT

Box 2 should contain all the things which will lead to high performance but which are not priorities on a day to day basis. These are the usual "I'll do it tomorrow" activities, which might cover:

- Journalling, reviewing, updating playbooks, analysing and assessing you, your systems, your strategies and tactics.

- Application of decision-making tools.

- Planning and strategising.

- Learning and development activities, coaching, mentoring, courses.

- Self-development activities.

- Taking breaks, monitoring time and reducing hours.

- Personal and mental wellbeing activities: getting fit, staying healthy, running or taking walks, gym work, diet, nutrition, hydration.

- Spiritual wellbeing activities: making time for your religious practices, mindfulness, meditation, yoga, time with family and friends.

BOX 3: THINGS THAT ARE URGENT AND NOT IMPORTANT

Box 3 will contain matters which you feel are urgent but not important. Disturbances, nuisance activities, and some of those activities you can outsource, accounting and finance, management of your investment portfolio (if it is not central to your work), perhaps even some analytical and research activities.

BOX 4: THINGS THAT ARE NOT URGENT AND NOT IMPORTANT

Box 4 will contain time-wasting activities, social media, time-killing activities.

Box 2 thinking is the devotion of time, energy and investment to the "I'll do it tomorrow" activities. These are the areas which will make you more productive, more effective.

Team Sky and Kermit Washington went against the grain and put extra effort into learning and development activities.

Kaplan and Massar insisted that their blackjack team members kept active logs of all their activities.

The trader in Tom Dante's story stayed late in the office reviewing his trades, even on very successful days.

Michael Jordan put in the extra hours training.

Amrit engaged in almost all the activities mentioned here.

Lisette reviewed all her poker activities, and did the same in her trading.

Rowen was an active journaller and planned his trades in detail.

Warren, Rowen, Amrit, Daljit, Tony, Lisette and all the elite performers mentioned in this book worked with a coach.

I could go on, but hopefully you have the point. Box 2 activities are the ones which develop your human potential and your mental game.

In your quarterly and annual periodic reviews, try filling out a Covey Matrix and reviewing which activities you are doing and where your time and energy is going.

You may find that you are spending too much time in Box 4, or you may notice that many of the activities that you think are Box 1 activities actually go in Box 3. You may realise that you are not planning, scheduling and doing enough Box 2 activities.

CIRCLES OF CONCERN AND INFLUENCE

During my coaching programme with Peter Burditt, he suggested that I was spreading my energy too thin by worrying about concerns outside of my control, which were little more than distractions. He introduced me to a model from Stephen Covey's *The 7 Habits of Highly*

Effective People (Simon & Schuster, 1989): the Circles of Concern and Influence. This model focuses attention and effort on factors that lie within your influence, thus helping to shift you from being reactive to proactive.

The model consists of two concentric circles. The Circle of Concern is the outer circle and represents all the things that were taking up my mental energy, but which I could not impact or control. The inner circle, the Circle of Influence, was a much smaller range of concerns that I could affect and control.

My Circle of Concern was filled with matters I was giving attention to that I could not influence, and soon began to squeeze into the space the Circle of Influence occupied, causing it to shrink. I realised that I was devoting a worrying amount of energy to external activities I could not control.

This metaphor helped me declutter my external Circle of Concern and focus on matters within my Circle of Influence, principally my trading process.

This had a big impact on me, and soon far more of my energy and focus went into my trading process, resulting in significantly more effective trading. I became more present to my process and purpose, and external concerns no longer took any of my energy or focus.

Focusing internally on my work paradoxically allowed me to indirectly affect some of the external concerns I was previously worried about.

This was also illustrated in the story of Kyle's behaviour slippage in Chapter 3. By focusing on his work, where he could influence matters, rather than worrying about his reputation, Kyle was able to improve his performance and close his performance gap, indirectly affecting his reputation as well.

Over time, I have come to see the Circle of Concern model in a different light. While you cannot directly change your external or internal world, you can focus on and change your process, which can positively influence and impact both. Your process is your Circle of Influence.

THE PRE-MORTEM AND DECISION-MAKING TOOLS

The pre-mortem is a tool used by project leaders and facilitators to help increase the success of projects and plans. It is the brainchild of psychologist Gary Klein, whom you may recall from Chapter 21's story of the firefighter.

I encourage clients to consider using the pre-mortem to help improve a range of aspects connected to their trading and investment performance, to help counter the negative effects of behavioural biases and to help improve decision-making.

Research has found that 'prospective hindsight' – imagining that an event has already occurred – increases the ability to correctly identify reasons for future outcomes by 30%. A 'pre-mortem approach' is a way of using prospective hindsight to help identify risks at the outset of a trading or investment performance.

The concept of a pre-mortem relies on getting a group of people to assess the potential reasons for the failure of an idea or plan. This is done as a group exercise. The exercise starts with a team being briefed on a project plan. They are then informed that the project failed spectacularly.

The team members are then asked to independently write down potential reasons for the failure. Then the team members are asked to read out one reason from their list until everyone has exhausted their list of potential reasons.

Afterwards a review process begins. The reasons offered are evaluated, and then participants discuss how they can strengthen the plan and make its success more likely.

This is a useful tool in many investment situations, but it naturally has limitations in personal situations where you are working alone. However, this does not mean that you cannot engage in pre-mortem-style thinking.

I used this often in my trades. I would come up with an idea, then think, "Okay, where could this fail?" I would bring out a list of my many usual tendencies: over-confidence, confirmation bias, self-doubt, hesitancy, over-risking, adding outside of my plan, tinkering and finessing to try and steal a few ticks, leaving stops too tight, not considering what approach this trade was, and many more.

This process helped me formulate more robust and tighter plans. It also drew my attention to potential alternative paths for trades, and alerted me earlier to when it became clear that a trade was not working. As a result I became far quicker to act, since I had considered these scenarios.

You will find further details of these frameworks on the website performanceprocesscycle.com, along with journalling tips, tripwires, and playbook construction.

I also highly recommend Annie Duke's book *How to Decide: Simple Tools for Making Better Choices* (Portfolio, 2020) which references a number of decision-making tools to help improve how we make choices in the face of radical uncertainty.

CHAPTER 36

That's a Wrap

To be yourself in a world that is constantly trying to make you something else is the greatest accomplishment.

Ralph Waldo Emerson, philosopher and poet

THIS BOOK WAS about *you*.

There is an idea I have referred to a few times throughout this book. It is that the market has an agenda: it wants your money, and it needs you to fail or unravel so that it can win.

It needs you to engage with it unprepared, ill-informed.

It needs you to carry the wrong map, and to believe that the map is the terrain.

It wants you to play all your chips when you are not experienced enough and do not have a deep enough understanding of what is needed to succeed.

The market requires you to be overconfident, to play from the perspective of a complicated world, to not play with a poker mindset and a business attitude.

It needs you to take it on when you are weak and tired.

It wants your ego to be its best ally and not yours.

It wants your ego to construct a self-image that you want to project in your trading, which your ego then seeks to defend, and which ensures you do not ask for help or find ways to be better.

It wants you to put your pride first, so that you can fall next.

It wants you to respond immediately, rather than chewing things over.

It needs you to get straight back in after being knocked back, rather than taking the full count.

It needs you, prompted by your ego, to play to the crowd.

It wants you to focus on winning now, so you do not strive to get better and grow stronger in the long term.

It does not want you to develop your human potential through activities which make you sharper, stronger, faster, better.

It does not want you to ask for help, enquire about help, consider help, seek help. It needs you to think that getting help is a sign of failure.

When you are lost and confused, the last thing it wants you do to is ask for guidance. It wants you to think you can do it all alone.

It needs you to sustain that challenging relationship you have with your self, not to repair it.

It definitely does not want you learning the under-appreciated art of self-compassion practised by those who are happy to be vulnerable and comfortable being uncomfortable.

Above all, it does not want you to let go of any of that. It needs you to hold on to all those beliefs you have, all the things you do which undermine *you*. It needs you to keep self-sabotaging, because that way it can own you, rather than you owning your own journey.

To do so, it first convinces you that you can take money from it by doing these things, and then when you try it relies on you unravelling. That is what the market wants for you.

The market doesn't just want you to go on-tilt, it needs you to go on-tilt.

It wants to throw you off the golden chariot which represents your process, it wants your ego to take over the reins of that chariot, with you helpless and abandoned on the side. The last thing it needs is you taking back the reins and having control.

The mental game empowers you to fight back. You can either help the market do its work, or you can do yours. This is up to you; you do have choices.

But the mental game cannot be won at the external level. You can make small adjustments and hacks which can have some impact, but most of the time they are sticking plasters – cosmetic solutions at best.

To maximise your chances of winning the mental game you must bring the real, true you to the fight. This is the strongest and most powerful version of you.

The world you were brought up in will have done all it could to change and modify you. It is possible that it has changed you so much that you have trouble recognising yourself.

The only version of you that can win, over time and in a way that you will be satisfied with, is the true you. This is a wise and highly capable version of your self that has almost unlimited potential. A version of you that you can truly identify with.

The fight back against the market starts by getting to know this version of your self, then getting to like it, respect it and value it.

In this book, the ego is portrayed as an entity almost separate from the self, but that portrayal was largely metaphorical. The ego *is* part of you, but it is a part of you which does not work in the way we have been taught to think. It is not the enemy, merely a feature of how we operate. The most powerful version of you is realised when you, your self and your ego are aligned and working towards a unified, wholesome purpose.

With this purpose defined, you can formulate a process to achieve this. You then need to be present to this purpose and the processes which make it possible. This happens at the boundary of the inner game and the outer game, where the mental game is played. This is where you ride your golden chariot.

The purpose of this book is to help you become a more self-informed, self-aware and self-confident individual as a trader, a performer, a person. I hope it inspires you to focus on looking inward and seeing all that is amazing within, so you can bring that to the external challenges you face, whether in the markets or in everything else that you do.

NOTES

1   Schwager, J.D., *Market Wizards* (Wiley, 2012).

2   Zuckerman, G., *The Man Who Solved the Market* (Portfolio, 2019).

3   Alexander-Passe, N., (2015). 'Perceptions of Success in Dyslexic adults in the UK' *Asia Pacific Journal of Development Differences*, vol. 2, 1, pp.89–111.

4   Al-Lamki, L., (2012). 'Dyslexia: Its impact on the Individual, Parents and Society' *Sultan Qaboos University Medical Journal*, vol. 12, 4, pp.269–272.

5   Hatfield, S., Hogan, S., Mahto, M. and Sniderman, B., (2022). 'A rising tide lifts all boats' Deloitte Insights. Retrieved from www2.deloitte.com/uk/en/insights/topics/talent/neurodiversity-in-the-workplace.html.

6   Mohoney, M., (2003). 'How Customers Think – The Subconscious Mind of the Consumer (And How To Reach It)' Harvard Business School. Retrieved from hbswk.hbs.edu/archive/how-customers-think-the-subconscious-mind-of-the-consumer-and-how-to-reach-it.

7   Essentia Analytics (2022). 'Research Paper: The Alpha Lifecyle'. Retrieved from www.essentia-analytics.com/the-investment-alpha-lifecycle.

8   Tierney, J., (2011). 'Do You Suffer From Decision Fatigue?' *New York Times*. Retrieved from www.nytimes.com/2011/08/21/magazine/do-you-suffer-from-decision-fatigue.html.

9   Golombek, D., Leone, M., Sigman, M. and Slezak, D., (2017). 'Time to decide: Diurnal variations on the speed and quality of human decisions' *Congnition*, vol. 158, pp. 44–55. Retrieved from www.sciencedirect.com/science/article/abs/pii/S0010027716302414.

10   Bechara, A., Damasio, A., Damasio, H. and Anderson, S., (1994). 'Insensitivity to future consequences following damage to human prefrontal cortex' *Cognition*, vol. 50, 1–3, pp.7–15. Retrieved from www.sciencedirect.com/science/article/abs/pii/0010027794900183?via%3Dihub.

INDEX

ABOUT
THE AUTHOR

Steven Goldstein is one of the leading coaches in the financial markets industry. He holds accreditations in coaching and organisational development competencies from several bodies including the European Association of Gestalt Therapists. Prior to becoming a coach, Steven worked for almost 25 years as a trader at some of the world's leading investment banks. His experience and know-how endow him with a unique understanding of financial markets, human behaviour, and performance development skills. This combination enables him to help people in trading and investment make powerful transformations that drive personal growth and improve bottom-line results.